Across Oceans, Into Forever

Seventeen Years of Love, Faith, and the K-1 Visa Journey

By
S.C. Beall

Copyright © 2025 by S.C. Beall
All rights reserved.

ISBN:
Paperback: 978-0-635-44681-7

No part of this book may be reproduced, distributed, or transmitted in any form or by any means, including photocopying, recording, or other electronic or mechanical methods, without the prior written permission of the publisher, except in the case of brief quotations embodied in critical reviews and certain other noncommercial uses permitted by copyright law.

To my wife, Arwa, the strongest, most accepting, and most caring woman I have ever met.

Table of Contents

Chapter One: Be Committed	1
Chapter Two: Expect the Unexpected	14
Chapter Three: In for a Penny, In for a Pound	16
Chapter Four: Living For the Long-Term Goal	19
Chapter Five: Forms, Forms, Forms	29
Chapter Six: Oh, the Waiting!	34
Chapter Seven: Double-Check	36
Chapter Eight: What Do We Do Now?	41
Chapter Nine: Prepare for Marriage (Remember that Commitment Thing)	47
Chapter Ten: Things to Consider	57
Chapter Eleven: You're in This Together	61
Chapter Twelve: The Long Road Ahead	65
Chapter Thirteen: A Plethora of Pitfalls	73
Chapter Fourteen: We Made It Through All That Other Stuff…Onward!	77
Chapter Fifteen: Final Thoughts	97
Acknowledgment	101
About the Author	102

Chapter One:
Be Committed

Welcome!

You are here because you need help navigating the K-1 Visa process. You made the right decision by picking up this book. By submitting specific documents to the United States Citizenship and Immigration Services (USCIS) and getting an approved K-1 Visa, you will have permission to bring your partner to the United States for 90 days and hopefully get married.

Then, you get to live happily ever after, right?

While that is technically true, the process is more complex than that. It requires something much more symbolic and influential than some pieces of paper. It requires commitment and staunch devotion.

This book is about the K-1 Visa process, but more importantly, your commitment to each other through thick and thin. It is about obligation across continents and borders, which requires you to remain faithful to your partner, even if separated by vast distances of land or oceans.

It is not your typical relationship, the one you see on TV shows, where a boyfriend and girlfriend spend plenty of time together, going on dates and watching movies. No, it is not straightforward. It can even push you to a point where you spend $1,500 on filing documents and possibly hiring lawyers that charge even more than that.

It requires unconditional financial commitment, which can easily call into question your integrity.

You may find yourself asking, "Is this the right decision?"

For me, it was 100% the right decision; I came out ahead in the deal because my wife is the kind of person that anyone would dream of having in their life. Not to brag, but she meets all the keywords that would come up if searching for the perfect partner in an imperfect world. Primarily, it is the fact that we ultimately accept and respect one another. We are not always perfect together. We have had our share of rough spots, mistakes, and miscommunication, but at our core, we are uncompromisingly committed to each other.

So, believe me when I tell you that applying for a K-1 Visa does not start with filling out a form; it begins long before that.

It begins with surety.

You must be entirely and firmly sure you want to do this. You want to be confident that your love for this person you are trying to get a K-1 Visa for extends beyond boundaries and knows no borders. Ask yourself, "Am I willing to do everything I can to get this person through this process so we can be together?"

Being steadfast is a crucial mental state required to initiate this process, as it is essential to address any unresolved reservations or concerns before proceeding.

Considering this, before we proceed to discuss the K-1 process, it is essential to understand the real challenges of maintaining a relationship with a foreign national. This book serves as a reality check for individuals who aspire to marry a foreign national, shedding light on the often-glorified, romanticized, and exotic concept.

Although there are a lot of flowers and sunshine, it is not always that way; it will change both of your lives forever. You must have the strongest will and dedication to your partner to survive this tedious journey; all of that must come before you even apply for a K-1 Visa.

Relationships across borders for an American (or anyone else, for that matter) must be something in which they have a genuine investment. These relationships require one to live through (possibly overlook, compromise with, or outright accept) many differences in the dynamics of their life compared to their partner's.

There is a possibility of a significant language barrier, as well as cultural and religious differences, and varying daily living practices. This kind of situation can be found anywhere in the United States, but regardless, being on the same soil helps communicate these differences.

But why does it all sound so negative? Is it that bad? Do I mean to sound pessimistic about this?

Well, no. It is not all negative; it is just challenging. However, going through the challenge will give you a more rewarding life experience than you could have ever imagined; it will open your eyes to a more incredible world beyond your bubble. It will help you understand the meaningful things in other people's lives.

Not everyone celebrates the same holidays as you, or, surprisingly, to some whom I have met, people in different countries also have access to the Internet, television, and all the other basic amenities of life that we hold dear here in the US. You would find your aperture opened to the bigger picture of the differences and similarities across many cultures.

Please know, however, that this book is not a guide on relationships. It is merely an insight into our experience. I will tell you about what I faced and how I felt as I applied for a K-1 Visa (and everything that came before it), as you might find yourself in a similar situation.

Hence, it is also essential for you not to take my experiences as empirical evidence, but know that much of what I write here holds universal truth. That said, it is merely my own, sometimes chaotic and beautiful life experience. Yours may be different, but you will find many similarities. The K-1 Visa process, for instance, might be similar, and the documents you fill out may be the same. Remember that every couple has different situations and requirements, which would be difficult to document in a single volume.

One important thing to understand, especially in the context of foreigners, is that people who live outside the United States sometimes have this utopian perception of life in the United States. Some of that may be dispelled by news and media outlets. Nonetheless, some foreigners still consider the U.S. a land where they would go, and money might fall from the trees. My wife had a similar impression. However, she soon discovered that things didn't exactly pan out as planned.

With this odd perception of America, many people believe they will come here, achieve great things, and make a fortune. It is not as easy as you might think. But remember this lesson:

success is achievable from nearly anywhere on this planet. However, wherever you end up, achieving financial success requires hard work, sacrifice, and maximum effort.

Being from the U.S. and being used to living here, I did not understand the dynamics of this misconception. Not fully aware of my wife's mindset, I agreed that getting a job and making a life was possible. Therefore, it is essential to note the following lesson: when bringing a foreign national to the US, you must understand that person's mindset and the type of experience they expect. Ask those questions. For example, a work Visa to the U.S. is different; that person is coming to work on a specific project or job, but with a K-1 Fiancée Visa, they are coming here to start a new life.

I met my wife while stationed at Camp Lemonnier in the Horn of Africa, Djibouti. I was about seven years into my naval career, and I happened (perhaps through divine intervention?) to be set up by a mutual friend of ours, whom we shall call…Tim. Tim absolutely insisted that I go to meet my future wife at the coffee shop where she worked on the base, called The Green Bean Cafe. Now, Tim is not psychic; he did not know we would get married, but he is pretty good at matchmaking. We were two people from very different walks of life, me, an outspoken, stubborn boy from Allen, Texas, and my wife, a coy, brilliant girl from Djibouti! We found ourselves quickly navigating a romantic, whirlwind relationship that involved me writing English-language love letters, which were then translated into French by my wife's Djiboutian friends who knew English.

As you can imagine, there was a lot of giggling, "tee-hees", bashfulness, and hopefulness. Well, after suffering the giggling, which wasn't much to suffer, really, I found that the base was offering a 10-week Conversational French class for service members on the base, and I thought, "Jackpot!" After finishing that French course, and believe me, I studied extra hard, I was finally able to communicate with this fascinating woman, whom I can now call my wife.

So, dear readers, this book is for anyone who has found a love connection like mine and wants that special person to join them in the U.S.. It could be someone who works in the U.S. and meets a random stranger while staying at a hotel in Acapulco, Mexico. That is the kind of thing I am talking about here. Remember, when watching TV shows like "90-Day Fiancée", the surprising part is that there is nothing special about the people in these cases. Just like you and me, they are ordinary people seeking a deeper connection with someone. They were either looking for love or not, and eventually met a fantastic person on their travels.

When you decide to take that relationship further with the K-1 Visa process, the U.S. citizen in the relationship must be transparent and honest with their fiancée about the potential difficulties of adjusting to American culture. I lacked in this area, thinking my wife could "figure it out"; looking back, I was very naïve. There were several things I could have emphasized more clearly to give my wife greater clarity. Seeing it from her perspective, I realized my mistakes and misunderstandings over the years, which is also part of why I wanted to write this book. I wanted to give people some insight into what can better prepare them for the endeavor they are considering.

To recap, I was a 30-year-old Navy guy (still a kid in some ways, if I am being honest in my self-evaluation), stationed in Africa after living in Hawaii, partying and living the single life for nearly ten years, and not thinking about what it meant to be in a committed relationship with somebody after all that time.

Mentally, I was ill-prepared for all the troubles that my wife and I would face during the whole process, but we made it work, mainly because my wife is one of the strongest people I know. She was able to cope with more hardships than I could ever have imagined.

A quick note for younger people who have grown up in the Reality TV era of relationships. Understand that you must separate the false "reality" of these TV shows from actual reality, where love, understanding, communication, and trust are paramount. Those shows are highly dramatized for entertainment and ratings, designed to draw you in and keep you watching the drama. Yes, the people in those shows may genuinely feel something about specific events, but you must remember that the cameras are rolling, and drama sells TV shows. And I do not recommend allowing that type of drama to invade the sanctity of your relationship. You must consider that you are asking this person, who has a life of their own, to assimilate into a different place, like the Borg from Star Trek (ok, maybe not that hardcore, but still…).

This brings me back to my wife and the things she expected that I genuinely did not fully understand at the beginning, and how my wife had to make too many sacrifices from my perspective, which, unfortunately, greatly hindered the process of assimilating into U.S. culture. Looking back, it would have been more tolerable with an actionable social support system. The minimal support and lack of consideration on my part at the beginning of our marriage, and the precedent it set, continue to cast a shadow on our past experiences as a married couple and occasionally affect our lives, even now. Which, as you can guess, dear reader, is another reason I wanted to write this book, and keep people from making these mistakes.

With that said, I would like to address another sensitive aspect of this process: social support, whether from friends or family. For example, if your family knows you plan to bring your significant other to live with you in the U.S., they might not provide any practical support, which can be very upsetting and create a lot of tension; this could be your reality. Everyone's family situation is different. Some people may have full support and active involvement with a positive interest in both of your life journeys. Others may only have people who support them from a distance, offering encouragement (and sometimes negative comments), but not much in the way of action. Still, others may receive no help at all.

Know that you cannot change how people choose to support you or your decisions, even though it will sometimes cause friction between you and your support group. Understand that those relationships are still meaningful; you have to say what needs to be said. Still, even if it hurts or has not fully reached reconciliation, do not wait too long to get to that point; those people still matter very much. Remember, you must take responsibility for your actions, not blame others, and do what is best for you, your community, and your family. Doing otherwise would lead you down a darker path, filled with regret and negativity, that would consume your life and possibly destroy the beautiful ride you are on with the incredible person you have met.

Remember, these are the lessons we (my wife Arwa and I) have learned over the years; they may or may not apply to you, but if they do apply to you, having a trusted family member or individual therapist who can offer professional support is one of the best options to navigate those waters. Trust me, those seas get choppy; stand by for heavy rolls.

As challenging as it is to navigate all that with your own family and support system, it is just as challenging learning each other's cultural differences. A notable difference between my wife's culture and mine in the U.S. is that her family had a full-time housekeeper or two who would assist with the daily tasks of running a large family. A housekeeper or full-time nanny may sound luxurious, but it was simply a matter of economic culture. Paid home-service labor is significantly cheaper in Djibouti; that is all there is to it.

However, that is not the case in America unless you are well-off! My family was middle-class, so they could pay for a maid service that came to clean the house once or twice a month. For many people in the US, even that is considered fancy, but that's about the extent, unless you are incredibly wealthy and can afford to pay $30,000 to $60,000 a year or more for a full-time caretaker or home assistance service.

This fact was a huge culture shock for my wife. Imagine being accustomed to a level of community and family that is always there to help you with day-to-day tasks and then coming to terms with the fact that you would have to do all that work by yourself. You genuinely must put yourself in her shoes to appreciate it. Open your mind's eye, and imagine a small family home, made of cinderblocks, with cool, glassy-smooth concrete floors, situated on the corner of two dusty dirt roads. The heat outside swelters to 109°F. Inside, there are three bedrooms, a bathroom, a family area, and a small kitchen. The father is the bread-winner, the mother is head of the house, some of the locals are hired to assist in the house, they become like a second family, as they cook and clean and help with child-rearing duties, your extended family lives in similar houses all around you, conversations and family issues are talked about in gatherings at one household or another, and all this at the cost of what equates to a single night's meal for two in the U.S. at a five-star restaurant, for the entire month. I know this because I was able to witness it, and experience a tiny part of it, and the fact that I had to write an Economics research paper for my undergraduate degree on the comparison of Gross Domestic Product per Capita using Djibouti and the U.S. as my compared economies (like what other countries would I use, right?) So, think about that: it's your whole life. Upon reflection, you realize what a significant change it is. So, as you imagine this and at the same time your perception of America is "luxury," then you can see how when you meet the reality of the U.S., it might be "underwhelming."

Now, do not get me wrong, as a retired Navy Chief, I know the U.S. is a proud land of independent warriors and entrepreneurs, including me, and I also know we can sometimes overlook how distant and detached the family unit in the U.S. has become compared to cultures that are so closely bonded and tight-knit.

With all this, I want to express the gravity of what you are about to undertake; either you or your spouse will leave a country, a home, a family, and friends, and journey to a new land. It is a highly daunting task. I advise you to immediately put yourself in that person's shoes (think of it from their perspective) and imagine every question you might have about a journey like that.

What are the demographics of the population? What are the tax regulations? Is my partner on good terms with their family? How easily can I get a job? Can I even get a job?

And a plethora of other questions that might apply to your unique situation.

El Guapo: "Would you say I have a plethora…"

Jefe: "Oh, yes, El Guapo. You have a plethora."

El Guapo: "Jefe, what is a plethora?"

Jefe: "Why, El Guapo?"

A little "Three Amigos" movie humor for you.

Trust me, it is a plethora, and it certainly applies to the questions you should be asking each other.

Your K-1 Visa journey is unique; those nuances and questions are essential. It truly boils down to your level of commitment, as you should be working consistently (at least once or twice a week) to review your paperwork and ensure everything is in order.

It is also vital that you start understanding their culture beforehand and provide them with insight into your own culture. Understanding each other's culture will help you better understand that person. If you have the means and time, go on some dates (in person, not online) beforehand to get to know the person more before making this decision (although that should be obvious; however, not all cultures are the same).

Back to our origin story…after meeting my wife at the Green Bean coffee shop on base at Camp Lemonnier, we got together as much as possible. I was a Navy Sailor living on a U.S. military base with a curfew, and she was a native of Djibouti. Everything was secretive and different from what I was used to in America.

It was like the "007" of dating (queue the James Bond theme music!) because it was taboo for the women in that culture to be out unescorted with a man not from their family or to date people openly. On what was supposed to be our first date, my wife did not even show up. I kept calling the number she gave me repeatedly, but there was no response. The next day, I met her at the coffee shop, asked what had happened, and she explained everything to me. She replied, "I gave you the wrong number on purpose to see if you would show up." This lady is brilliant, street-smart, attractive, and knows five languages.

Sign me up!

In my mind, she was asking if I was committed to her. After that, we went on an actual first date and continued for the next six months. The moment I knew I was all in was after taking the French language course and learning as much French as I could. So, now I know quite a bit of conversational French; not fluent, but decent. Taking that step with someone I had just met in a foreign country convinced me that I was ready to commit to the relationship. At the end of my time there, I asked her if she wanted to come to America. To my delight, she agreed.

That is where I started finding out what kind of paperwork was required for this K-1 Visa, especially since I was in the military. Still, there were many things I did not know about her and her culture. Especially the way her family placed so much emphasis on ensuring their families were involved in everything. It was an obligation to ensure that everyone was cared for, whether in terms of health or finances. There was a very communal aspect to her family and neighbors that was new to me, and it made me realize, as I have witnessed this over the years, that we have lost a lot of that here in the US.

Hopefully, introducing our story will help you consider your possible experiences in the K-1 Visa process. It is much more than a bunch of paperwork. It encompasses this rich history between you and your partner. Along the way, I hope to help you understand that you must expect the unexpected while undergoing this process and remember the phrase **"control what you can control; do not worry about what you cannot control."**

More importantly, you cannot control how people react to this decision. Never expect someone who has lived in another culture their entire life to assimilate quickly into your society here in the U.S.. That way of thinking is highly selfish and a recipe for disaster. Give yourself and your partner time to adapt to and accept this life decision. Remember that nothing is guaranteed in these relationships, but staying committed and open-minded can lead to better success and satisfaction.

Chapter Two:
Expect the Unexpected

The K-1 Visa process isn't just about paperwork — it's a journey full of curveballs, surprises, and "you've got to be kidding me" moments. If you think it's going to be smooth sailing, buckle up. This is more like crossing the Atlantic in a dinghy with one oar and a leaky floorboard.

I'll never forget when my wife's father passed away while we were still in the green card stage. She was in her third trimester, couldn't fly for the risk to the baby, and was grieving thousands of miles away from her family. There was no form one could file to fix that. Nothing can be fixed when the world drops from beneath your feet. No magic USCIS stamp to make it easier. Just love, endurance, and a lot of prayer. That's when I realized the most important rule of this whole process: **expect the unexpected.**

The Honeymoon Phase Trap

Falling in love is wonderful. But making life-altering decisions when you're starry-eyed can backfire. The "honeymoon phase" is not the best mindset for tackling immigration law. Trust me — marriage is more than roses,

FaceTime calls, and whispered promises across time zones. If you don't balance romance with realism, the surprises will flatten you.

Lesson: Uncertainty Is the Rule, Not the Exception

Unexpected pregnancies, emergencies, financial shocks, and cultural traditions you didn't see coming are common. They are not a matter of if, but when. Your goal isn't to avoid them but to prepare your relationship so it can withstand them.

Practical Tips: How to Prepare for Surprises

- **Discuss Cultural Norms Early:** Ask about family traditions and expectations. (Example: My wife's culture includes a 40-day recovery period after childbirth. In the U.S., three weeks of leave felt like a luxury.)
- **Budget Beyond the Basics:** Have an emergency cushion. Costs will come up that you never thought of — trust me.
- **Know the Visa Rules:** The K-1 Visa is single-entry. If your fiancé leaves before marriage, the marriage becomes invalid. Research Form I-131 for emergencies.
- **Plan Weddings Smartly:** Use the long wait for planning. The 90 days are for execution, not brainstorming.
- **Expect Emotional Highs and Lows:** Homesickness, fear, and even grief are natural. Your role is to be a steady partner, not a fixer.

Takeaway

Every K-1 journey is unique, but none are without surprises. Don't treat setbacks as red flags. Treat them as tests of your resilience as a couple. If you can weather the unexpected together, you're already winning.

Chapter Three:
In for a Penny, In for a Pound

Let's talk about money. Love may be priceless, but the K-1 Visa process isn't. Filing fees, medical exams, travel, and legal help add up quickly. In 2007, I paid about $1,000. Today? Try three times that amount before you even reach the wedding cake.

Here's the thing: the costs aren't just financial. They're emotional, cultural, and sometimes spiritual. But since the bills hit your wallet first, let's start there.

Paperwork Costs

- **Form I-129F (K-1 petition):** $675
- **Form DS-160 (State Department processing):** $265
- **Medical Exam:** $100–$500
- **Form I-485 (Adjustment of Status):** $1,440
- **I-765 (Work Permit, with pending I-485):** $260
- **I-131 (Advance Parole):** $630

That's about $3,270 before you purchase the first bouquet. And remember — errors can lead to refiling, which means paying again. Double-check everything. (See Chapter Seven:

Double-Check.)

Travel & Housing

Airfare isn't cheap, and once your fiancé arrives, you'll need a stable place to live. Living with your parents? Probably not the best plan. At least have a backup arrangement. And don't assume "one-bedroom in Manhattan" when a modest place in the suburbs will do.

Living Expenses

Utilities, groceries, healthcare, transportation — all of these will increase once you're living together. And don't forget cultural differences: maybe your fiancé(e) only eats halal, or avoids pork, or misses the taste of home. These little things have hefty price tags if you're not prepared.

Cultural Costs

Some expenses aren't listed on any government website:

- **Dowry expectations** (in some cultures, very real).
- **Wedding costs** (both American and abroad).
- **Traditions** like jewelry, gold, or gifts for family.

I paid a dowry for my wife. It wasn't about the money — it was about respect for her culture. That respect matters more than the dollars.

Lesson: Count Every Cost, Not Just the Obvious Ones

The most significant costs aren't always financial. They're emotional adjustments, cultural sacrifices, and lifestyle changes. But planning for the financial side makes space to deal with the rest.

Practical Tips: Managing the Money

- Budget at least $4,000–$5,000 beyond what USCIS lists. Hidden costs are inevitable.
- Book flights early, during off-peak seasons.
- Have open, honest talks about lifestyle expectations. Luxury there doesn't always equal affordability here.
- Keep a shared budget. Both partners should know where the money's going.
- Don't forget health insurance. In the U.S., that's not optional.

Takeaway

Love is worth every penny, but don't fool yourself — this process can be costly. Plan, budget, and brace for surprises. Your wallet may be lighter, but your relationship will be stronger.

Chapter Four:
Living For the Long-Term Goal

One common issue couples encounter during the K-1 Visa process is that they view it as a linear progression from not having a visa to obtaining one, essentially from point A to point B. This is a false perception of the whole thing because there are many points in between, and, more importantly, life after the visa matters the most. It is essential to plan for life. Let's look at some things that couples tend to overlook.

Adjustment Period: Understanding the Cultural and Emotional Adjustments Both Partners May Face:

Entering a new country and adapting to a different culture is a significant transition that is often overlooked. For the foreign fiancé(e), moving to the United States means leaving behind familiar surroundings, family, and friends, which can lead to isolation or homesickness. Simultaneously, the U.S. citizen partner must adjust to new dynamics in their relationship and daily life.

Cultural Adjustments:

Every country has its unique customs, traditions, and social norms. These differences can be both fascinating and bewildering. For instance, holiday celebrations, food preferences, and social etiquette may vary significantly. Understanding and respecting these differences is crucial for both partners.

Simple interactions, such as greeting strangers or tipping at restaurants, might be new experiences. Being patient and open to learning can ease this transition.

Even if the foreign fiancé(e) speaks English, the way a U.S. citizen speaks English may differ in context. This means that idiomatic expressions and regional accents can pose challenges. Engaging in language learning activities together, such as watching movies or practicing daily conversations, can be helpful.

Emotional Adjustments:

Missing family and friends is natural. Establishing a routine for regular communication with loved ones back home through video calls, social media, and in-person visits can help alleviate some of these feelings.

The foreign fiancé(e) may experience a sense of loss regarding their cultural identity. Please encourage them to maintain cultural practices and celebrate their heritage, creating a sense of continuity and belonging. Push yourself to take an active role in their heritage as well.

Due to the various changes, both partners may feel stressed. It is essential to recognize these emotions and address them through supportive conversations or seeking professional help if needed.

Building a Support System: Finding Local Communities, Support Groups, and Resources for Immigrants:

Creating a local support system is healthy for the post-visa period. A strong network can provide emotional support, practical assistance, and a sense of community, making the transition smoother for both partners.

Local Communities:

Many cities have cultural centers or community groups for specific nationalities or ethnicities. These centers often offer social events, language classes, and other resources to help immigrants connect with others from their home country.

Churches, Mosques, temples, and other religious institutions can offer a welcoming community and support for newcomers. They often host social gatherings, charitable activities, and educational programs.

Support Groups:

Join local or online support groups specifically designed for immigrants. These groups can offer advice, share experiences, and provide a platform for discussing challenges and solutions.

Many areas have networks for expatriates that organize social events, professional networking opportunities, and other activities to help newcomers integrate into the community.

Resources for Immigrants:

Many local governments offer resources for new immigrants, including information on housing, employment, and legal assistance. Checking local government websites can reveal a wealth of helpful information.

Numerous nonprofits focus on immigrant support, offering services ranging from legal advice to language classes and job placement assistance.

Community colleges and adult education centers often provide language courses, cultural orientation classes, and other programs to help immigrants adapt to their new environment.

Communication: Strategies for Maintaining Open and Honest Communication in Your Relationship:

Regular Check-Ins:

Make it a habit to talk about your day, share your thoughts, and express your feelings, no matter how small and inconsequential they may seem. This routine can help you stay connected and understand each other's experiences and emotions.

Set aside time each week to discuss any issues, plans, or changes. Use this time to review your goals, address concerns, and celebrate achievements.

Active Listening:

Give your partner your full attention when they speak. Avoid interrupting or planning your response while they are talking.

Try to understand your partner's perspective and feelings. Acknowledge their emotions and validate their experiences, even if you do not entirely agree.

Expressing Feelings and Needs:

Use "I" statements to express your feelings and needs when discussing sensitive topics. For example, say, "I feel stressed when..." instead of "You make me feel...".

Honesty is crucial, but it is also essential to be considerate. Frame your concerns in a way that encourages constructive dialogue rather than defensiveness.

Problem-Solving Together:

Approach problems as a team. Use phrases like *"Let's find a solution together"* to let them know you are in this together. Be willing to compromise and find a middle ground. Understand that both partners may need to make concessions to reach a mutually satisfying solution.

Seeking Help When Needed:

If communication becomes difficult or strained, consider seeking help from a professional counselor or therapist. They can provide tools and strategies to improve communication and resolve conflicts. Joining support groups for couples in similar situations can also provide additional perspectives and solutions.

Changing Perspectives Over Time

Personal Growth:

Entering a new country and maintaining a cross-cultural relationship brings various experiences and challenges that can significantly alter your viewpoints and your bond with your partner for better or worse. Our goal is to make sure it is for the former.

As you grow together, your goals and values may evolve. As mentioned earlier, regularly discussing your aspirations ensures that both partners remain aligned and supportive of each other's personal and professional development, helping to deepen your bond.

Relationship Dynamics:

As you settle into life together, your relationship dynamics will naturally evolve. Initially, one partner might take on more responsibilities to help with cultural adaptation or language barriers, but it is important to reassess and balance these roles over time.

Career changes and job opportunities can also impact your relationship, requiring mutual support and balance. Increased intimacy and constructive conflict handling are healthy ways to maintain a relationship.

Then, there is the question of starting a family. Prepare for these changes by discussing parenting styles and responsibilities and establishing boundaries to help maintain harmony and respect in the relationship.

Setting Long-Term Goals:

The secret behind any lasting relationship is prioritizing long-term goals. Differentiate between short-term and long-term goals, and identify which goals are personal and which are goals you are both striving towards.

Regular check-ins to review and adjust your goals as life circumstances change, ensure that both partners remain motivated and aligned. Financial planning plays a significant role in achieving these goals. Setting monetary goals for savings, investments, and major purchases and creating a plan to achieve these goals helps maintain financial stability. A financially unencumbered relationship is usually a happy one, which brings us to the next point.

Financial Realities and Unexpected Expenses

Budgeting:

Track all monthly and annual expenses, including housing, utilities, groceries, transportation, and insurance. Compare your total household income to your expenses, ensuring that your costs do not exceed your income. Allocate a portion of your budget to an emergency fund to cover unexpected costs, such as medical emergencies or job loss.

Review your budget regularly to ensure you are staying on track. Adjust as needed to accommodate changes in income or expenses. Discuss these changes and keep your partner informed. Finances should always be a group decision in a relationship.

Travel Costs:

Travel expenses can be significant, especially when visiting family in another country. Planning and budgeting for these trips is essential. Please set up a travel fund (especially if you are in a relationship that crosses borders and continents!) and contribute to it regularly to spread out the cost of travel over time.

Book flights and accommodations well in advance for lower prices and better deals. Traveling with children can be more expensive, so plan for these increased costs and look for family-friendly travel options that offer discounts or unique amenities for children.

Hidden Costs:

Unexpected expenses can strain your budget if you are not prepared. Identify potential hidden costs and plan for them beforehand. Ensure you have adequate health insurance coverage for all family members and understand what your policy covers.

Maintain a fund for medical emergencies to cover unexpected healthcare costs. If you or your children plan to pursue further education, be sure to account for tuition, fees, books, and other related expenses.

Budgeting for extracurricular activities, such as sports, music lessons, and school trips, can increase over time. Regularly save for home and car repairs to avoid financial strain when unexpected issues arise. By doing all this, you are working towards establishing something stable and long-lasting.

Balancing Life's Complexities

We obviously cannot forget about the day-to-day workings of a relationship. Sometimes, these little things can make or break a relationship.

Work-Life Balance

Achieving work-life balance is essential for overall well-being. Prioritize tasks by identifying the most important and setting clear boundaries between work and personal life. Allocate quality time for family and relaxation to prevent burnout and maintain healthy relationships. Simple strategies, such as avoiding work emails during family time and scheduling regular breaks, can help you stay focused and present at work and home.

Parenting

Being a good parent and partner requires effort and coordination. Share parenting responsibilities to ensure that both partners are involved and supportive. Create a routine for family activities and one-on-one time with your children. Additionally, make time for each other as a couple to strengthen your relationship. Regular date nights or simple, uninterrupted conversations can help maintain a strong partnership amidst the demands of parenting.

Health and Wellness

Maintaining your health goes hand in hand with managing your relationship. If you are physically and mentally at your best, you can give your partner your best. Incorporate regular physical activity and healthy eating into your daily routine. Simple changes, such as walking more and eating balanced meals, can have a significant impact on your overall health. Recognize the signs of stress and burnout, and do not hesitate to seek professional help. Practices like meditation, pursuing hobbies, and ensuring adequate rest can support mental well-being and help you stay resilient. My wife and I each have our own interests that occupy some of our time, and we make time to pursue those things on our own. We give each other a break from the stresses of parenting and feeling overwhelmed at home.

While looking out for the "big things" is essential in the K-1 Visa process, couples often overlook the minor, day-to-day things. If overlooking becomes a habit, it can create problems for the future, so treat everything with balance and consideration. Remember, *all things in moderation.*

It is a lot to remember, but that is what life becomes when you step into something as monumental as getting married, especially when it involves someone from another country, and even more when it comes to having children. That person also has a responsibility to you in these ways. It is always a two-way street. Ensure you are fulfilling your end of the agreement.

S.C. Beall

Chapter Five:
Forms, Forms, Forms

Forms, forms, forms!

Just the thought can be enough to make anyone's eyes glaze over. I understand it is an extremely tiring and tedious procedure, but let's face it: paperwork is a fundamental part of the visa process. Whether you are someone who meticulously organizes every document in a color-coded folder or struggles to remember where you last saw your passport, understanding why these forms are crucial can help make the process less daunting and even more tolerable.

First off, why are forms so important?

Think of forms as the structured language of bureaucracy. They provide a standardized way to present your information, ensuring that all necessary details are captured accurately and efficiently. While organizing all the information you need in a singular place can be challenging and tedious, you will appreciate it once it is done.

When it comes to something as significant as the K-1 visa, the accuracy of your paperwork can make or break your application. These forms are the primary means by which U.S. Citizenship and Immigration Services (USCIS) and consular officers assess your eligibility, intentions, and the authenticity of your relationship. They might seem tedious, but they are your gateway to a new life together in the United States.

Completing these forms diligently and correctly will streamline your application process and demonstrate your seriousness and preparedness to the authorities. This helps to build a positive impression and can significantly reduce delays and complications down the line. So, as much as you might dread the paperwork, it is worth taking the time to get it right.

Focus and Diligence

Filling out forms is an art form in itself. While that may sound unusual, like any art form, it requires focus, patience, and a bit of creativity. The creativity part comes in when you must figure out how to fit your life's story into tiny boxes.

Start with a quiet, clutter-free workspace. Gather all your essential documents: **passports, birth certificates, previous visa documents, and any other relevant paperwork.** It is much easier to fill out forms when you have all the necessary information right in front of you. Use a checklist to ensure you do not miss anything. Remember, missing information can lead to delays or even denial of benefits.

Take your time. Rushing through forms increases the chance of mistakes. Double-check names, dates, and numbers to ensure they are accurate and correct. USCIS and other immigration authorities are thorough; even a small error can cause considerable delays. When unsure, do not hesitate to ask for help or clarification. There are many resources available, including official guidelines, community forums, and legal advisors.

Essential Forms for the K-1 Visa

Now, let's get into the nitty-gritty of the specific forms you must fill out for the K-1 visa. This section will cover the essential forms, namely Form I-129F and Form DS-160, two critical documents for your visa process.

Form I-129F: Petition for Alien Fiancé(e)

The Form I-129F, Petition for Alien Fiancé(e), is your starting point. The U.S. citizen submits this form to USCIS to establish their relationship and intent to marry. Here is a breakdown of what you need to know:

1. **Basic Information:**

Begin with your basic information, including your name, address, and contact details. Ensure these match your official documents exactly.

2. **Biographical Information:**

You will need to provide details about your fiancé(e), including their full name, date of birth, and place of birth. Double-check the spelling and dates.

3. **Evidence of Relationship:**

This section is crucial. You must provide evidence that you've met in person within the last two years. This could include photographs, travel itineraries, and any correspondence. Be thorough but concise.

4. **Intent to Marry:**

Both parties must sign a statement of intent to marry within 90 days of the fiancé(e)'s arrival in the U.S. This is where you show your genuine commitment.

5. **Additional Documentation:**

Attach the necessary supporting documents, such as passport copies, photographs, and proof of U.S. citizenship. Make sure everything is up-to-date and legible. Remember, if something is in a foreign language, it will need to be officially translated! **Do not forget** to **translate** everything and get translators for interviews! Also, add translation fees to those **extra costs!**

Once completed, review the form meticulously. Any errors or omissions can lead to delays. When satisfied, submit it along with the required filing fee to USCIS. After submission, you will receive a Notice of Action (NOA1) acknowledging receipt of your petition.

Form DS-160: Online Nonimmigrant Visa Application

After USCIS approves the I-129F petition, it is time for your fiancé(e) to complete Form DS-160. This online visa application form will be submitted to the U.S. Department of State for a consular interview.

1. **Starting the Application:**

Visit the Consular Electronic Application Center (CEAC) website. Then, select the appropriate location where the visa interview will take place.

2. **Personal Information:**

The form will request extensive personal information, including full name, nationality, and marital status. Ensure that all entries are accurate and match the information on your passport.

3. **Travel Information:**

Provide details about your travel plans, including your intended arrival date and U.S. contact information. If your plans are not finalized, provide your best estimate.

4. **Passport and Travel History:**

Enter your passport details, including the passport number, issue date, and expiration date. Also, provide information about any previous U.S. travel.

5. **Security and Background Information:**

Answer a series of security-related questions honestly. These cover a wide range of topics, from criminal history to previous visa denials. Be truthful, as any discrepancies can result in denial.

6. **Review and Submit:**

Once all sections are completed, review your answers carefully. After submission, you will receive a DS-160 confirmation page with a barcode. Please print this page, as it will be required for your visa interview.

Staying Organized and Prepared

Organization is vital throughout this process. Create a dedicated folder for all your immigration documents. Keep copies of everything you submit and any correspondence you receive from USCIS or the consulate. This will help you keep track of your progress and provide a quick reference if you need to resubmit any information. Later, we will discuss common form-filling mistakes and guide you on how to avoid them.

Completing immigration forms can be overwhelming, but remember that each form you complete brings you one step closer to starting your new life together in the United States. Stay focused, stay motivated, be diligent, and do not hesitate to seek help when needed.

Chapter Six:
Oh, the Waiting!

If you're reading this, you've probably already learned that immigration has its own timetable. Spoiler alert: it's slow. The waiting is the hardest part. In fact, it might be the most formidable challenge of all.

For my wife and me, the process lasted 11 months. Eleven long months of refreshing websites, checking mailboxes, and wondering if our paperwork had disappeared into a black hole. Patience wasn't just a virtue — it was survival.

The Reality of the Wait

On average, the K-1 process takes 6–9 months. However, delays can occur due to backlogs, global events (such as the COVID-19 pandemic), or even minor mistakes on your forms. You may feel helpless at times, but behind the scenes, things are still moving.

Lesson: Patience Is Part of the Process

Waiting doesn't mean nothing is happening. It just means it's not happening on your timeline. If you can't handle waiting, you'll struggle with marriage as well.

Practical Tips: Surviving the Wait

- **Stay Busy:** Use the downtime to prepare documents, plan your wedding, and save money.
- **Build Connection:** Schedule regular calls or visits (if possible). Use the time to strengthen your bond.
- **Work on Culture:** Learn each other's language, food, and traditions. The wait is a perfect time for this.
- **Stay Healthy:** Exercise, eat well, and keep your mind occupied. A healthy you is better for your partner, too.
- **Find Support:** Join online groups of others in the K-1 process. You'll realize you're not alone in this.

The Test of Time

My wife and I went through grief, culture shock, and separation during our wait. But each day brought us closer to forever. Looking back, the wait wasn't pointless. It helped us slow down, communicate more effectively, and prepare for life together.

Takeaway

Waiting is part of the K-1 journey — frustrating, yes, but necessary. Instead of fighting it, embrace it. The months you spend waiting can become months you invest in building a stronger foundation. The paperwork may end, but the patience you develop will carry into your marriage.

Chapter Seven:
Double-Check

The Dangers of Making a Mistake

Regarding the K-1 visa process, even the slightest mistake can have serious consequences. When you think about it and read it here, it might seem obvious that "of course, I would double-check everything. No one needs to tell me that." I have a lot of personal and professional experience with this, first in handling the K-1 Visa process myself, and second as a Navy Chief who has spent hours correcting and rewriting my mistakes and spelling errors, as well as those from Sailors who thought they had it right. I did not, and they did not. Some errors were obvious if you just took two seconds to read what was written.

Errors on your forms can lead to delays, requests for additional information, or even outright denials. Trust me when I say you do not want to receive that "Denial" or "Rejected" message in the mail. This happened to us once on one of our documents because there were small details out of place, such as a box that was not checked. That is why this chapter is crucial to reiterate: double-check your submissions to USCIS. Going through the process in the first place is already a stressful time for couples, so any delays or errors due to simple mistakes can be extremely frustrating.

Given the significant time, effort, and emotional investment involved, ensuring accuracy and precision from the outset is essential. Mistakes can happen to anyone, whether a simple typo, an incorrect date, or a misunderstanding of the form's requirements. Therefore, it is essential to understand the potential pitfalls and take proactive steps to avoid them. Remember, *preventative maintenance is better than emergency repair.*

The Importance of Double-Checking

Double-checking is a good habit and a necessary step in the visa application process. After spending hours, days, or weeks gathering information and filling out forms, it is easy to overlook details due to fatigue or familiarity. Reviewing your application with fresh eyes or after taking a break can help you catch errors you might have missed. Think of double-checking as your safety net, ensuring your hard work is not wasted.

Remember, try to avoid haste at all costs. I understand that it can be highly tempting to speed through and complete the forms quickly, but it is always better to take more time to recheck everything. It's no joke when I say USCIS will find any excuse to reject the package and have it resubmitted for perfection. They look at it as if they have provided you with instructions, and you failed to follow them. But that is their job, to weed out those unwilling to go the distance to ensure their K-1 Visa is perfect. It's a gauntlet, and you must have the fortitude to endure.

What to Look Out For

Here are some key points to consider when double-checking your forms for the K-1 Visa process. These details might seem simple, but are often easily overlooked:

1. **Personal Information:**

Ensure that all names, dates of birth, and addresses are accurate and consistent with the information on your official documents. A minor discrepancy here can cause significant issues. TRANSLATE EVERYTHING!

2. **Supporting Documents:**

Verify that all required supporting documents are included and correctly labeled. Missing or incorrectly labeled documents can lead to delays.

3. **Signatures:**

Make sure all necessary signatures are present. Forms without required signatures will be returned, causing delays.

4. **Dates and Deadlines:**

Verify that all dates are accurate, particularly for travel history, relationship timelines, and filing deadlines. Incorrect dates can raise red flags.

5. **Completeness:**

Ensure no sections are left blank unless explicitly instructed to do so. If a question does not apply, write "N/A" (Not Applicable) rather than leaving it blank.

6. **Financial Information:**

Double-check income figures, tax information, and any financial affidavits. Accurate financial information is crucial for demonstrating your ability to support your fiancé(e). I mean, if you did not realize that before, I hope you do now! You must be able to support them, not in a transactional way; it should help them, not be something held over them or against them. You are doing this with love and respect. This all goes back to what was said in the beginning and is a difficult concept for some Americans to understand. This is about transformational concepts, becoming a married couple, and growing together, not tallying up receipts for the future!

Should You Have It Checked by Someone Else?

After you have reviewed your forms, having someone else look at them can be beneficial. A fresh pair of eyes can spot mistakes you might have missed. This could be a trusted friend, family member, or, ideally, a professional. Immigration attorneys and accredited representatives are well-versed in this department, and they can help you look over things that you might have missed and catch errors that might not be obvious to you.

Friends and Family:

While they may not be experts, they can still help identify apparent mistakes or omissions. Choose someone detail-oriented and trustworthy.

Professional Help:

Hiring an immigration attorney or accredited representative can be particularly beneficial. They can guide you, ensure all forms are filled out correctly, and assist you with any other complex process. This, however, is a costly option as well.

Online Resources and Forums:

Participating in online immigration forums can also be helpful. Many people share their experiences and tips, which can provide additional insights into what to watch out for.

Remember, double-checking your application ensures a smooth K-1 visa process. By meticulously reviewing every detail and enlisting the help of others, you can significantly reduce the risk of errors and increase your chances of a successful outcome.

Taking the extra time to double-check now can save you months of delays and frustration later. Do not think of the whole thing as a tedious task; treat your pathway to a future *(together)* with the care and attention it deserves.

I cannot stress this part enough; listen to that feeling you get just before you seal those documents to be sent in the envelope. If you feel confident that all has been checked, *t*s crossed, and *i*s dotted, seal that envelope and send it to your required USCIS location for review. But if you get a little butterfly feeling in the pit of your stomach, stop there, *take a breath*, pull those papers back out, and CHECK AGAIN that all those documents are in order.

Your life and your partner's life documents are in this envelope, and you must get them right. Do not hesitate to check again. And do not think that you are being too cautious; one small error can reject the whole package. However, do not worry; once you have checked, double-checked, and reviewed it, it is time to seal the envelope and send it out for success!

Chapter Eight:
What Do We Do Now?

You've managed to navigate through the long and intricate visa process, and now it is time to look ahead to the final steps before acquiring your K-1 visa, as well as what comes after that life-changing moment.

Let's discuss some crucial final preparations, such as the visa interview process and what to expect once your visa is approved. We'll also discuss the key milestones you'll need to focus on after arriving in the U.S., including obtaining a Green Card, working toward permanent residency, and ultimately, achieving U.S. citizenship.

Final Preparations Before the Visa Interview

The visa interview is one of the most critical steps in the K-1 visa process, and proper preparation is crucial. Here's how to ensure you and your fiancé(e) are fully ready for this last stage.

1. Gather All Required Documents

Before the interview, ensure you have all necessary documents organized and readily available. This typically includes:

- *A valid passport for the foreign fiancé(e)*
- *Copies of Form I-129F (the initial petition)*
- *Form DS-160 (Nonimmigrant Visa Application)*
- *Evidence of a genuine relationship (photos, correspondence, travel receipts, etc.)*
- *Financial documents from the U.S. citizen sponsor, including recent tax returns and the Affidavit of Support (Form I-134)*
- *Birth certificates, divorce decrees, or death certificates if applicable*
- *Police certificates from countries where the foreign fiancé(e) lived*
- *Medical examination results*

Ensure you have multiple copies of each document and that they are organized in a clear and accessible manner. You do not want to be fumbling for paperwork during the interview.

2. Preparing for the Interview Questions

The consular officer's primary goal is to verify the authenticity of your relationship, so expect to be asked questions about how your relationship developed and your plans. Be prepared to provide details like how you met, the timeline of your relationship, and any significant milestones. Focus on being honest and detailed in your answers, like mentioning trips taken together, shared experiences, and family interactions, which can add credibility. It is also essential to show that you understand each other's daily routines and long-term goals, reinforcing the seriousness of your commitment.

Potential questions could include:

- *How did you meet?*
- *When and where have you seen each other in person?*
- *What do you plan to do after you are married?*
- *What do you know about each other's families, interests, and daily lives?*

Honesty is critical. The consular officer wants to see that the relationship is genuine and that both partners are committed to building a life together.

3. What Not to Say in Visa Interviews

Avoid vague or inconsistent answers. Any hesitation or conflicting information can raise red flags. Do not try to provide answers you think the officer wants to hear. Fabricating details can lead to denial. Never appear uncertain about basic facts such as significant dates or plans for your life together. Refrain from discussing intentions to stay in the U.S. outside of the visa parameters (e.g., working on a tourist visa), as this could imply you're trying to circumvent immigration laws.

4. Managing Pre-Interview Anxiety

Pre-interview nerves are natural, but staying organized can help ease stress. Having all your documents in order, such as passports, photos, and proof of relationship, will give you the confidence you need. Rehearsing answers with your fiancé(e) can also help you feel more at ease during the interview. The key is to stay calm, focus on the positive aspects of your relationship, and remember that the interview is just one more step in the process.

After Visa Approval: What's Next?

Once the visa is approved, it is natural to feel a wave of relief, but it is also essential to understand what comes next. The K-1 visa allows the foreign fiancé(e) to enter the United States, but this is only the beginning of the next stage in your immigration journey.

1. Entering the United States

Upon entering the U.S., the foreign fiancé(e) has 90 days to marry the U.S. citizen petitioner. During this time, it is crucial to finalize any remaining wedding preparations, but do not forget that there are also legal steps you'll need to take.

2. Filing for Adjustment of Status

Once married, the next significant step is filing for an **Adjustment of Status (AOS)** to obtain a Green Card. This will allow the foreign spouse to live and work in the U.S. permanently. The AOS process involves submitting Form I-485 and supporting documents, including a marriage certificate, evidence of your ongoing relationship, and financial documentation.

Remember that until the foreign spouse receives their Green Card, they will need special work and travel permits if they wish to work or leave the country temporarily.

3. More Interviews: Green Card

In some cases, USCIS will schedule a Green Card interview to confirm the legitimacy of the marriage. Much like the K-1 visa interview, the Green Card interview focuses on the authenticity of your relationship. Be prepared to provide further documentation and answer questions about your life together as a married couple. It is essential to remain patient during this phase, as receiving the Green Card can take several months to a year.

Long-Term Plans: Citizenship and Beyond

After the Green Card is acquired, there are additional steps to consider, especially if you want to pursue U.S. citizenship. Although this process may seem distant, it is crucial to plan.

1. Applying for U.S. Citizenship

To apply for U.S. citizenship, the foreign spouse must first become a permanent resident (Green Card holder). They will be eligible to apply for citizenship after three years of permanent residency, provided they are still married to the U.S. citizen petitioner. This is done through the **naturalization** process, which involves passing a citizenship test on U.S. history and government, demonstrating proficiency in English, and meeting specific residency requirements.

2. Keeping Immigration Documentation Updated

Throughout your immigration journey, staying on top of all paperwork and documentation is vital. For example, Green Cards must be renewed every 10 years, and you'll need to file the necessary forms if you change addresses or encounter any changes in your marital status. Maintaining a good immigration status ensures that you avoid unnecessary complications and difficulties.

3. Preparing for Life After the Visa Process

It is easy to get so focused on the visa and immigration process that you forget what happens next. However, remember that you have an entire life ahead of you, for which you need to plan. Let us examine this further.

Chapter Nine:
Prepare for Marriage (Remember that Commitment Thing)

Keeping Your Eyes on the Prize: The Importance of Preparing for Marriage

As you navigate the K-1 visa process, it's easy to get caught up in the paperwork, interviews, and waiting periods. However, it is crucial to remember that the K-1 visa is not just a bureaucratic hurdle, but a significant step in building a life together with your partner. This process, although complex, serves a purpose, and that purpose is your marriage—a lifelong commitment that requires thoughtful preparation and dedication. The visa is not just a formality, but a significant milestone in your journey towards marriage. Since the Visa process is complicated enough, we can often forget that planning a marriage is equally, if not more, difficult.

Preparing for marriage is not just about planning a wedding. It is about laying the foundation for a strong, healthy, and enduring relationship. The transition from engagement to marriage involves significant emotional and practical changes. This chapter will help you focus on building a future grounded in love, mutual respect, and shared goals, which will bring you joy and fulfillment.

Why You Need to Prepare for Marriage

Marriage is not just a significant milestone; it is a profound commitment that shapes the rest of your life. It is a promise to support, cherish, and grow with another person, no matter what life throws your way.

While love and passion are the bedrock of any marriage, they are not the sole pillars that uphold a lifelong partnership. Preparation is vital to ensure your relationship can withstand the challenges and changes that inevitably come with time. It is this preparation that will enable you to stand by your partner in sickness and in health.

Understanding Commitment

Marriage is not just a change in legal status; it is a lifelong commitment to another person's well-being and happiness. It is not just a piece of paper; life before and after marriage is separate, yet those times are still part of your beautiful story. It is about being there for your partner, not just during the joyful moments but also during those difficult times. With all its beauty, this commitment inspires and motivates us to be the best partner we can be.

This commitment requires an understanding that marriage involves making sacrifices, compromises, and putting your partner's needs alongside your own. Preparing for this level of commitment means having honest conversations about what being a partner truly means. It is about recognizing that marriage is a partnership, where both individuals are equally responsible for nurturing and sustaining the relationship. By deepening your understanding of this commitment, you will be better equipped to navigate the inevitable ups and downs of married life.

Dealing With Cultural and Lifestyle Differences

In an increasingly connected world, it is common for couples to come from different cultural or lifestyle backgrounds. While this diversity can be helpful to your relationship, it also requires careful preparation to ensure that these differences do not become sources of conflict.

Discussing traditions, expectations, and lifestyle choices before marriage is essential. This preparation allows you to identify potential areas of misunderstanding and find ways to integrate and celebrate each other's cultures within your relationship. It is about creating a shared life that respects and honors both backgrounds, strengthening your bond and making you more resilient. By preparing for these differences, you can turn potential challenges into opportunities for growth and connection. Remember, no challenge is beyond communication.

Financial Planning

One of the leading causes of stress in marriage is financial issues, and rightfully so. Whether it is differences in spending habits, debt management, or long-term financial goals, money matters can quickly become a source of tension if not addressed early on. Preparing for marriage means having open and honest conversations about your financial situation.

For me, credit card debt has always been a lingering burden. You get it under control, and then a new expense comes up. It is a vicious cycle. Now that I am older and earn more, managing and reducing costs is much easier, and I can keep up with them more quickly. However, unless you are financially stable and have more money than you spend, debt will always be a part of the adult experience in this reality. Your job in this regard is to ensure you take care of the essential bills and debts *before* you spend money on *"wants"* or *"nice-to-have"* items. Maintaining that mindset will bring you comfort and contribute to a tranquil marriage. In my opinion, if your partner doesn't see the value in this and insists on paying for extravagant things that are well outside your budget, then they likely don't care about you or your relationship and are only looking out for themselves.

Discuss your current financial standing, including debts, assets, and income. This also involves setting mutual financial goals, such as saving for a home, planning for children, or building a retirement fund. Creating a budget together is a practical step that helps ensure you are both on the same page financially. Addressing financial matters before marriage reduces the likelihood of money-related conflicts and builds a stronger, more united front when managing your finances as a couple.

Setting Expectations

Every individual brings their own set of expectations into a marriage, shaped by their upbringing, previous relationships, and personal beliefs. These expectations can range from how household responsibilities are divided to how conflicts are resolved. Discussing these expectations before getting married is crucial to ensure that you are aligned with your future vision.

Discuss your views on roles within the marriage, how you plan to handle disagreements, and what your long-term goals are as a couple. By setting clear expectations, you avoid potential disappointments and misunderstandings. This preparation enables you to build a marriage founded on mutual understanding, respect, and shared goals, rather than assumptions and unspoken desires.

In essence, preparing for marriage is about more than planning a wedding. It is about laying a solid foundation for a partnership that will last a lifetime. By taking the time to understand the commitment you are making, dealing with potential cultural and lifestyle differences, planning your finances, and setting realistic expectations, you are setting yourself up for a marriage that is not only successful but also deeply fulfilling and meaningful, one where you can start a family and see your kids grow up in front of you.

Tips for Wedding Preparation:

Planning a wedding can be one of the most exciting things you can do with your partner, and the memories you create will last a lifetime. However, it can also quickly become one of the most stressful times of your life if you do not communicate properly and understand each other's positions and requirements.

Amidst the whirlwind of decisions and details, it is essential to focus on what truly matters: celebrating your love and commitment. Here are some tips to help you navigate wedding planning with ease and joy.

Start Early

One of the best ways to reduce wedding planning stress is to start as early as possible. Begin by setting a realistic budget and a timeline for when each aspect of the wedding needs to be finalized. Sit down with your partner and discuss what's most important to both, like the venue, the guest list, or your honeymoon. By identifying your priorities early on, you can allocate your time and resources more effectively, ensuring that the most essential elements of your day are precisely as you envision. Starting early also gives you a cushion to handle any unexpected hiccups without feeling rushed or panicked.

Keep It Simple

Weddings often come with societal pressures to create a grand spectacle. Still, it is essential to remember that this day is ultimately about your love and commitment, not about impressing others. Focus on what is meaningful to you and your partner. Whether that means having an intimate gathering with close family and friends or a more significant celebration, make choices that reflect who you are as a couple. Simplicity can often be more potent than extravagance; when the day is about your love, it will be memorable for everyone involved.

Delegate Tasks

Delegation is what helps Fortune 500 companies stay alive, and it will also help you avoid many sleepless nights. You do not have to do everything on your own. Planning a wedding involves countless details, and trying to manage them yourself can lead to unnecessary stress. Delegating tasks to trusted friends, family members, or a wedding planner can help alleviate this stress.

This lightens your load and allows those who care about you to be involved in your special day. Make sure you and your partner are both actively involved in the decision-making process. After all, it is a day for both of you, and having shared responsibilities will make the day feel even more meaningful. Remember, asking for help is okay; it is your day, and you deserve to enjoy it.

Focus on the Ceremony

While the reception often steals the spotlight with its elaborate setups and entertainment, the ceremony is the heart of your wedding day. This is when you and your partner will make your vows and commit to each other for life. Take the time to craft a ceremony that is personal and meaningful. Whether you opt for traditional vows or write your own, ensure that the ceremony reflects your unique relationship and the promises you make to each other. Personal touches, like including meaningful readings or involving loved ones in the ceremony, can make this moment even more special.

Plan for the Unexpected

No matter how meticulously you plan, something unexpected may arise on your wedding day. Whether it is a sudden change in weather, a vendor running late, or a minor wardrobe malfunction, being prepared to handle surprises gracefully is vital to maintaining your peace of mind. Have a backup plan for critical elements, such as the ceremony location or transportation, and be prepared to adapt to changes. Remember, the most crucial goal of the day is to get married. If you can keep that in perspective, everything else will seem less significant. Sometimes, the little imperfections are what make the day uniquely yours.

Take Care of Legal Requirements

Amid the excitement of planning, do not overlook the legal requirements of getting married. Ensure you apply for your marriage license well in advance and familiarize yourself with the legal requirements in your state or country. This is particularly crucial if you are getting married in a location different from where you currently live, or if you and your partner are from other countries. Ensuring all legalities are in order will prevent any last-minute complications and allow you to focus on enjoying your day.

Enjoy the Moment

Getting caught up in the to-do lists and stress of wedding

planning is easy, but enjoying the process is essential. This is a unique period in your life, filled with anticipation and excitement. Whether it is a quiet evening discussing your future together, a spontaneous date night, or a day spent picking out wedding attire, savor these moments. They are a part of the journey toward your wedding day and the life you are building together. When the day finally arrives, you will find that the memories you created during the planning process are just as unique as the wedding day itself.

For Arwa and me, our wedding day was one debacle after another. Neither of our immediate family members was able to come to our wedding, which still stings a bit, especially when I say it out loud. However, it wasn't entirely anyone's fault; the timeframe was short, just 90 days, and I could have done more planning and preparation. I spoke with my brother about it, and he reminded me of several circumstances that had contributed to that situation. Those conversations helped me realize some of my communication failures during those times, which only reinforced my desire to share this story with readers like you, so that you might avoid similar situations. I want you all to learn from our mistakes.

We initially went to the Justice of the Peace (JOP) in San Diego, CA. I was wearing my Summer White Navy Uniform, and she was dressed in a beautiful, floral-patterned Somali dress with high heels and a striking yet subtle floral headpiece that made her look stunning. However, despite our appearance that day, when we arrived at the building and stood in front of the JOP, she asked if Arwa could understand the marriage contract, which she could not. I asked the JOP if they had a French translator available, and was quickly informed that they did not. Then we were told we were supposed to have arranged that, another thing I had not thought of or known. After learning French and being able to read it, I asked the JOP if I could read it to Arwa, but she said it was a conflict of interest, which, of course, it was.

Frustrating was the word of the day. So, we could not get married that day, and it was a sad ride home.

We did not give up, though; I immediately contacted friends to help and found that a good friend of mine, Jesse Altillio, could speak and translate the French version of the marriage certificate for Arwa! So, we gathered Jesse and other friends, and we all headed to Point Loma the next day, driving down towards the beach area below the Cabrillo National Monument. When we pulled into the park, I asked the Park Ranger at the gate if marriages and ceremonies were allowed on the beach; he said they were allowed, but there was a three-month waiting list!

Well, I said "thanks for the information", and we drove down to the beach anyway, with Arwa in a different but still beautiful dress and me in business attire; we held hands on that gorgeous beach, said our vows, and my friend Jesse read that marriage contract in French and repeatedly asked if Arwa understood the words, which she did. My friends filmed it for us, but sadly, the video was lost over time. Arwa and I signed our marriage contract *(which was not lost!)*, and Jesse signed it as a witness! We still have that marriage license today with his signature. Now, 17 years later, looking back, I wish I had known and done things differently, had better advice and direction, or sought that advice more fervently than I did. I thought I knew all the angles and requirements, but I did not, and that is another reason I am writing this book for all of you who might be on this journey. Learn or do not, and you may have a crazy story like that to tell one day.

The main reason I wanted to tell that story is to immortalize and pay respect to my good friend Jesse Altillio, who battled with depression, attention-deficit/hyperactivity disorder, and insomnia after leaving the Navy, and unfortunately chose to leave this world on his own terms during the writing of this book in February 2024. He was a good man and a friend over the years, and his passing was not the sum of his life; if there was ever a song that defined who Jesse was as a person, it is the Steve Miller Band's "The Joker". "I'm a picker, a grinner, a lover, a sinner, I play my music in the sun. I'm a joker, a smoker, a midnight Toker, I sure don't want to hurt no one." That was all Jesse for sure. And he is why Arwa and I could continue our journey together and why we were able to bring our three beautiful girls into this world. So, thank you, my friend; I love you and miss you dearly.

In closing this chapter, I would like to emphasize the importance of mental health and focus on what truly matters. Approaching your wedding preparations with joy and collaboration can help ensure that your wedding day is beautiful and reflects your love and commitment.

Chapter Ten:
Things to Consider

We are in the final stages of our Visa journey. Now is when you and your partner will start to see the light at the end of the tunnel. You should not relax entirely just yet, but rest assured, you are closer to your future life with your partner than ever.

Now, we will take a comprehensive look at the essential tips and best practices you should consider. We have discussed most of these topics in greater detail, but it would be beneficial to review them here briefly.

These tips are intended to help you showcase your relationship and preparedness, demonstrating to the consular officer that you meet all the requirements for a K-1 visa.

Proof of Communication

One of the most essential elements to demonstrate is consistent and genuine communication between you and your partner. Consular officers will want to see that the relationship is both ongoing and sincere. Gather any relevant records of communication, such as:

- **Messages and Emails:** Screenshots or printouts of text messages, emails, or social media exchanges showing regular contact.

- **Call Logs:** Records of phone or video calls can help illustrate consistent interaction.
- **Photographs:** Pictures taken together during various visits or events are essential. Choose a range of images that reflect different moments, from casual days to special occasions, as this variety shows a more realistic portrayal of your relationship.

It is wise to be selective and avoid overwhelming the officer with too much. Instead, focus on quality over quantity, such as demonstrating genuine, meaningful communication that highlights your connection.

Proof of Financial Stability

Financial stability is crucial in the K-1 visa process because it reassures the U.S. government that the foreign fiancé(e) will not become a public charge. Here's what to prepare:

- **Bank Statements:** Recent bank statements showing a stable financial situation.
- **Employment Verification:** A letter from your employer verifying your employment and income can be helpful.
- **Affidavit of Support (Form I-134):** Completing this form is a formal way to show your ability to support your fiancé(e) financially. This form, along with supporting documentation such as pay stubs, tax returns, and bank statements, will serve as the backbone of your financial proof.

If any red flags arise during the financial review, address them honestly with the consulate. Being transparent about your finances demonstrates that you are upfront and committed to responsibly navigating the visa process.

Proof of Travel and Visits

In-person visits are a requirement for K-1 visas, with rare exceptions, so showing proof of these visits is essential. Use these items to confirm your time spent together:

- **Travel Itineraries and Tickets:** Flight bookings, boarding passes, and itineraries can serve as primary evidence of in-person meetings.
- **Hotel Reservations:** If you stayed together during trips, receipts from shared accommodation are good empirical evidence.
- **Passport Stamps:** Passport stamps showing entry and exit dates confirm physical presence, helping establish the timeline of your relationship.

Ensure that your documentation aligns with your timeline, as discrepancies could raise questions during the interview.

Additional Considerations

In addition to communication, financial stability, and travel proof, here are some other elements that can strengthen your application:

- **Joint Plans and Commitments:** Shared plans, such as moving arrangements, career goals, or even tentative plans for a future family, can illustrate your dedication to building a life together. It is helpful to discuss how each of you envisions your shared future.
- **Understanding Each Other's Backgrounds:** Demonstrating familiarity with each other's personal histories, family backgrounds, and interests shows you have taken the time to know one another deeply.

Tips for Presenting Your Documentation

Here are a few tips to help you organize and present your evidence clearly:

1. **Stay Organized:** Keep all documents in clearly labeled folders or envelopes so that you can access them easily during the interview.
2. **Be Prepared to Explain:** Avoid memorizing scripted answers during the interview. Be yourself and share your relationship genuinely.
3. **Avoid Overly Intimate or Irrelevant Details:** Stick to meaningful exchanges and avoid sharing overly personal details or conversations that might be seen as irrelevant.

Chapter Eleven:
You're in This Together

Where to go from here?

This is truly a journey that is only beginning. If you have the fortitude to stay true to your chosen path, then this journey will be excellent indeed. That is not to say that all will be roses and rainbows, but as the years pass and you genuinely come to know each other and learn from one another, you will find yourselves along the way. You will gain a culturally rich and much more enlightened way of living. I have developed a deep empathy for those outside my narrow scope since I was younger. I have developed more patience and learned new languages. After 12 years of studying and research, I decided to adopt my wife's religion and revert to Islam. I have opened myself to greater acceptance of my family's needs. I have become less selfish and more driven to excel, striving to learn from those past lessons and do better, to provide for my family and be a comprehensive leader.

Things will always need constant care within this unique relationship, but I feel that makes both of us strive to be better. There are still things we disagree about, and there are still those sore spots that stem from past choices, but there are also bright spots that highlight a life well-lived so far. It is a life I would not trade for anything, and I would do what is necessary to protect and cherish it. Whatever those things are for you and your partner, my dear reader, you will also know them as you face the challenges of a true union, a bond built upon your trust in each other.

As I stated before, trust is the foundation upon which a relationship like this must be built. Without trust, you will have nothing; I genuinely believe this. Trust in relationships today is challenging, especially when someone gives up their old life to build a new one with you. Whether in the U.S. or their country, you must trust each other. We can see from examples in shows like 90-Day Fiancé that when couples fail to trust each other or give their partner reasons not to trust them, the entire relationship will ultimately fail.

To build this trust, you must possess a strong will and a steadfast commitment. You must become self-aware of how your actions impact your partner, and you must be able to communicate and rebuild trust if either of you falters or makes a mistake.

And, yes, you will make mistakes, you will experience miscommunication, and face adversity as you build this bond. One of the best ways to overcome adversity is to be true to yourself, not try to be something you are not, and be honest with yourself and your partner. But in being honest you must be open to compromise, I know that this will sting, and your pride will take a few hits along the way, but this can never be a one-way relationship, sometimes that is the hardest thing to achieve as one of you may have more of an advantage based on where you live or how successful your career might be.

All these things must be considered if you are to succeed; you must put forth the effort to help each other accomplish what each of you wants to do in life. There are also great examples to follow and learn from. Ultimately, you and your partner must work together, motivate each other, and take calculated risks to achieve a shared life that you can both thrive in and look back on fondly.

I understand that sometimes things are too complicated, there is not enough support, or one of you cannot handle both good and bad times. It is a tough road, but you must keep looking forward. Do not let those failures or tough times define the core of the relationship. Deep at the core, you must be able to touch upon the strength of your bond with one another. That's the thing you should focus on to get through those more difficult times. Also, when taking the risks of a relationship, ensure you thoroughly evaluate the pitfalls and avoid going unthinkingly into something that might jeopardize your household.

Often, placing too much emphasis on something you want for yourself could potentially harm you or your partner and lead to the breakdown of the entire relationship. Ensure you can afford what you need first, such as shelter, food, and necessities. Making those essential things the focus of your efforts will put you in a better position to undertake more risky ventures, either together or separately. Each of you has your own goals, talents, and pursuits you want to follow; allow each other to pursue these things, encourage one another to do so, and support each other.

Ultimately, you must accept the choices that each of you makes in this relationship. Yes, you want to encourage each other, as I said, but if one or the other of you is pursuing a particular path, then also remember not to judge that too harshly. It is okay to be critical and disagree, but be open to listening to your partner when they explain their choices. Hopefully, for both of you, those choices are not detrimental or harmful. Hopefully, they will give you satisfaction.

Sometimes you will disagree with these choices, especially if they break that foundation of trust. I hope I don't need to explain this point further; I assume you understand what I mean. But for anyone who needs it straightforward, I am talking about cheating on your partner. Although my wife and I have had outsiders try to infringe on our relationship, we were fortunate to know and trust each other as our foundation, and we were able to fend off those attacks relatively easily. However, that situation was not without real stress and moments of doubt for both of us; we are just human beings after all, but seeing through people's bullshit is a lot easier when you know who your partner is and trust them at the very core.

Chapter Twelve:
The Long Road Ahead

With nearly 18 years of marriage now, it has been a life-changing journey. It started in Djibouti, Africa, because I wanted to do something else in the Navy. I wanted to see more and reach for more in life. Not that I knew I would meet my future wife and learn to speak French and ultimately decide to change my faith to Islam, it was just something I felt I needed to do at the time to further my career in the Navy, get away from the mundane ship life that seemed like one long Monday. Oh, yes, being in port in foreign lands and experiencing foreign cultures were welcome reprieves and amazing experiences that I would highly recommend to anyone feeling lost at a young age.

I'll take a moment to elaborate on the notion of feeling lost; I was lost at a young age, and as a young artist in the early days of digital art. In 1999, I was attending Collin County Community College to pursue a career in graphic design, and I learned a great deal from that experience as an artist. But at 20 years old, being in the same town for so long and having some of my advertising campaign artwork get rejected in my Business Advertising classes. And being told by professors that sometimes the businesses you work for or contract out for as an ad campaign designer are not going to like your first, second, or third submissions! Which, to me, at the time, was a "kick to the shins" in my pursuit of the art career I wanted. I couldn't see myself redoing meaningful artwork for an ad campaign at such a rapid pace, which might lead to an early grave due to stress.

So, I chose a career in the Navy, which is perhaps more dangerous and sometimes even more stressful, as it involves serving on warships that go out to sea and possibly into harm's way! I know it's hilarious to think about, but the Navy's stress, as I later discovered, was a burden shared by the entire team. Individuals were stressed, but we were usually in it together. Additionally, the Navy was going to allow me to leave my hometown, my parents' house, and live on my own, with a means of supporting myself and the care provided by the Navy, which would grant me further freedom. Of course, the Navy does expect payback in blood, sweat, tears, strength, grit, brains, and willpower; it demands those things from you and pushes you to sink or swim, literally. Much more than you realize is expected of you. Not all those expectations are written in black and white; they are written on your heart, mind, and in your bones.

Despite the challenges, I welcomed it; I had never been truly motivated to excel until I joined the Navy. It was as if a switch had been flipped; my parents had tried to motivate me to do well in school, but it never clicked until I joined the Navy. Every school and test I ever did in the Navy I did my best to excel at because it was my choice to do it, it was my life hanging on my performance, some people need that, I certainly did, and if you reader are out there feeling the same way, unmotivated and stuck, and if you meet the requirements then I would say join the armed forces in some capacity, it will change your life and outlook forever, especially if you give it all you have.

Now, there are no guarantees with that, it is challenging for most people to stick out 20+ years in the military, but you will find yourself very rewarded in life for having done so, going through the bad times and rough learning curves, to the physical danger that is present almost daily, with a few exceptions like shore duty areas and schoolhouses where the threat is minimized.

Ultimately, making that choice to join the Navy, signing up for the Delayed Entry Program, and then finally shipping off to boot camp in March 2000, when I was 21 years old, set me on the path to meeting my future wife, with whom I've now been married for almost 18 years. With our three daughters as well, and a new career that has allowed me to provide very well for my family after 22 years in the Navy, it was all worth it. Every hour on watch, every late night, every sleepless night, every emergency from 9/11, 2001, and that response through Force Protection Delta, to emergencies on the ship, from fires and the sewage pipes in the toilets exploding and leaking into our sleeping quarters. Through being berated by senior officers for speaking disrespectfully (which did teach me a valuable lesson in terminology, but was still kind of bullshit) and facing the tragedies of losing shipmates in the line of duty or to other causes, not that I wanted to see those shipmates pass on, but I believe those experiences were all worth it, as they pushed me to excel and reach where I am today.

So, again, if you find yourself there doubting your future, then it is worth a shot at least in the military, you never know that one day you could meet your wife overseas while on duty in Africa, after being forcefully encouraged by your fellow shipmates, or your own version of Tim, to pursue your own person that works in the coffee shop, depending on who you are and your situation in life. Never let an opportunity pass by, and always listen to your heart. It will ultimately lead you in the right direction and put you on the correct path.

As we work back into the K-1 process, I want to emphasize a point of rightness, properness, and correctness. I know from years of working with people from all backgrounds that everyone's home training on manners and ideas of right from wrong varies slightly. However, there is a way to determine if something is correct immediately, and it doesn't matter who you are; it is a universal truth. *If the thing you are doing seems hurtful or disrespectful to the person you are doing it to, would you want that same thing to be done to you? How would you feel if the thing you are doing, which you may think is fine to do to someone else, were done to you? Would you appreciate it?*

Just ask yourself those questions, and if the answer is 'No, I would not want this done to me,' then you probably should not be doing it to someone else. It is the Golden Rule: **Do unto others as you would have them do unto you.**

With that statement, we return to the K-1 Visa journey with your chosen partner. Now, many of us have seen 90-day fiancée, and I have mentioned several times how some of those individuals seem to treat each other with utter disregard, yet demand that the other person treat them with dignity and respect, while offering none in return. This may make for good TV drama, but it is no way to treat your partner. It is tragic if you think that way, that you are somehow owed all the respect while completely disrespecting the other party. You need to reevaluate your moral compass if you look in the mirror and see that this is how you behave.

At the beginning of this book, I stated that it is not intended to be a guide on relationships; rather, it is a reflection of my own experiences and observations from my journey with my wife and family. However, in that regard, you can take some honest advice: people often sabotage their relationships because they fail to look in the mirror and ask, 'What am I doing wrong?'

They are not being honest with themselves if they fail to recognize their actions, such as cheating or misusing their life partner's money, and using it for something other than what they initially intended. Now to be clear this is not something my wife and I ever had an issue with, my wife was God's way of saying to me that hope exists for the world and that if we all cared for each other the way she cares for her family in Africa and us as her married family here in the U.S., then the world would be a way better place to live in for everyone.

This advice on taking a deeper and more complex look at *your actions* comes from observing other relationships that I have encountered or witnessed over the years, not only in my life but especially in the fake bullshit drama that you see on a show like 90-day fiancée. Never treat the person in your life the way they are portrayed on that show. Be upfront, honest, and, above all, aware of your impact on that person's life, especially if they are the one who is leaving everything behind to be with you. You cannot be selfish in that kind of situation and still expect something good to come from it; doing that will ruin everything.

So, take it easy, feel it in your heart that this is the right thing to do, and if you feel that…correctness, that *"Je Ne Sais Quoi"*, that you are doing the best you can to honor and respect the other person in your life, then you are likely on the right path. Most of all, do not lie to yourself and then perpetuate that lie to everyone around you who can see that you are just spouting off bullshit. You are just lying to yourself if you say that what you are doing is fine when you can see that it is hurting your partner emotionally, mentally, physically, or financially. We all know lying and never acknowledging your uncaring actions is much worse. You never asked yourself, *"Why am I doing this to someone who does not deserve this treatment?"* And for you, dear reader, if you must know, much of this stems from the 90-day relationship between Gino and Jasmine, to be honest, from the get-go, the worst couple pairing in the universe!

DO NOT BE LIKE GINO AND JASMINE!

I could go on for days on that subject as my wife and I watch the show together sometimes, and some of my friends out there know the show as well, but for me, I cannot tolerate it for very long, and I must walk away, as I cannot fathom how either of them could have ever been seriously into each other. I can see why Gino would initially be drawn to Jasmine, given her sexy Latin vibe. Still, as soon as she opens her mouth or acts on her ambitions, all that **"¡Ella tiene esa sensualidad latina!"** *instantly,* as in *at the speed of light,* evaporates into raging evil queen vibes. And for Jasmine, she must have initially been like, Oh, what a sweet guy this Gino, and then when he opens his mouth, all of that completely evaporates as well, just two people that the universe never should have put together, in my opinion.

But what do I know about cosmic collisions of interstellar particles? Not much except what I learned from Carl Sagan, Stephen Hawking, Neil deGrasse Tyson, Janna Levin, Hakeem Oluseyi, David Kipping, and Brian Cox, to name a few of my favorite planetary scientists, astrophysicists, and particle physicists.

To recap, do not be like Gino and Jasmine. They underhandedly sabotage each other. They are a notable example of what not to do, especially when dealing with someone immigrating from one country to another. The callousness and audacity of someone acting selfishly in that situation are reprehensible at best.

There was a trend of people saying *"YOLO!", You Only Live Once, or Live Your Best Life.* However, when you have decided to involve someone else in that life and especially, someone from another country, who you have become involved with to the point you are considering going through the K-1 Visa process, it is now incumbent upon you to be responsible toward that person in regards to their needs as well, many times throughout this book I have mentioned compromise. I am sure many people in this world today do not understand the whole meaning of that word; they are so focused on this *"take care of my needs"* kind of attitude that they completely forget or ignore that they have this other soul in their life that also needs nurturing, caring, and love.

To the best of your ability, acknowledge that a partner exists in your life, not just recognize them, but celebrate, yield to, and make them part of your priorities, your number one priority in this worldly realm. Now, I do understand that sometimes it will feel like you cannot or are not doing a good job of this, because believe me, I have had my moments where my career took over my life even after marriage, and sometimes it is that way, otherwise you could lose that career if you do not show up and get the job done, that is when your partner also has to yield to you, knowing that you are doing what you are doing because ultimately you are focused on providing that safety and comfort and security. That there is a roof over our heads, clothes on our backs, and food in our bellies. That truly comes from my heart because I've felt it many times, being away from my family in the Navy while they are back at home, wondering why it must be this way.

It is difficult, and anyone in a career field that takes them away from family, even for short periods, understands that struggle. But again, do not sabotage each other. Understand each other, embrace each other's needs, and accommodate those needs as best you can. If you always try to do that, you will find a way through any pitfalls.

Chapter Thirteen:
A Plethora of Pitfalls

Speaking of pitfalls, my wife and I have experienced plenty, some of which I have hinted at throughout this book, and a pitfall is a trap you are not prepared for and suddenly snares you into a pit, full of some kind of nonsense, such as poisonous creatures, spikes, or boiling acid. You choose your adventure on that one. But believe me, sometimes you will think something is a good investment, only to realize it's not. Sometimes you'll miss out on something that was a good bet. Sometimes tragedy strikes a family member unexpectedly. Many of those situations have taxed our lives, but we have fared well and kept strong through the years, for the most part. Pitfalls await everyone, and many hesitate to commit to another person because their actions might affect them.

However, the fear of failure can drive and motivate us to overcome challenges and succeed. No one can truly be prepared, as unexpected disasters always arise. I could pack all the survival gear into my fallout bunker, but if the asteroid hits near that bunker before I can get in, then that preparation was all for nothing. My point is that you and those you care about most will face pitfalls of untold proportions. Still, you cannot live life fearing those pitfalls; you must take those risks to gain reward, like I did when my wife first touched my arm when we initially met behind the Green Bean Coffee Shop. You need to follow where that path leads, no matter what, especially if you are a grown adult who can make adult decisions for themselves.

Live your life and take others with you in the best way possible. Be a motivator, a beacon, and take some risks. Be open to discussion and that ever-present compromise. No one goes through life alone; there is always someone who cares about you, whether it's friends, family, or others. Very rarely do we have a superhero backstory where our parents died in a tragic accident, and we were orphaned and inherited a bat-cave.

Now, there are those folks out there for whom that situation may be true, and I acknowledge your tragedy if that is you; even so, they have someone in their life. And we should feel obligated to improve the lives of those who positively affect ours. The negative people and naysayers in our lives *"can go straight to a nice time, on a lonely beach in the middle of winter"*, to say it nicely. However, those who positively impact us and are willing to help us navigate the pitfalls and endure government-imposed processes, such as the K-1 Visa process, deserve our very best, even in the face of our fears of failure. We should do everything we can to make life as amiable as possible.

You should not be afraid to take that chance when lightning strikes, as it did with my wife and me, which, again, funny enough, she remembers in a completely different way. Be that as it may, I was not thinking of the pitfalls; I only thought, *"I need to learn French, so that I can speak to this lady!"* Pursuing my wife was the right choice; our connection proved it over the years. Despite the differences in our cultures, personalities, and upbringings, I believe this meeting was inevitable in my life. My decisions had led me here, and my nagging friend Tim, who insisted I meet her, bless him, played a role as well.

Pitfalls are inevitable; face them together. Commit to supporting one another, giving each other space when needed, and embracing the good times with open arms. Look at what your heart says, I had to learn that over the years, I could not understand that until I had the time to process it, I knew that what I had was worth saving and fighting for and to be the best person I could for that incredible blessing I had been given in meeting this wonderful person that I get to call my wife. Those who know her know what she is about; we know how much she cares and wishes that things could be perfect, and she does her best to make things perfect. Even if they are not always, they are still in my mind.

If you don't feel that way, be honest; stringing someone along because you fear the consequences is also harmful and worsens things in the long run. All relationships take work and everyone adapts to them in their own time, but if you just do not have that feeling of connection or desire to connect, then be open about it, going through the K-1 Visa process is not a thing to take lightly, and if you can see it is not going the way you thought, stopping it sooner rather than later is better.

This kind of relationship dynamic requires a concerted effort from both partners to cultivate a shared vision of their lives together. It is not about one person bending entirely to the will of the other, but about both individuals finding ways to grow alongside one another. True partnership is a balance of autonomy and unity. It is a dance where both individuals lead and follow at different times, depending on the rhythm of life.

When two people reconcile their differences and harness their strengths, they become an unstoppable force against the pressures of the outside world. Conversations become the cornerstone of this effort, as no issue can be resolved without clear communication. It's about creating a space where vulnerabilities are not shamed but embraced, dreams are not dismissed but nurtured, and challenges are not feared but navigated together.

Moreover, the importance of shared rituals and traditions cannot be overstated. Whether it's a weekly coffee date, a nightly stroll, watching 90-day fiancé together, or simply sitting down for dinner without distractions, these moments act as anchors in the swirling tides of life. They remind you why you chose each other in the first place and offer the emotional fuel needed to face whatever lies ahead. Ours is me making morning coffee and bringing it to my wife. I am forever trying to correct the coffee balance; one day, I will get there, but the thought counts. So, pitfalls be damned, deal with them as they arise. Do not let them stop what could ultimately be a life-affirming and long-lasting relationship that alters the course of your life for the better.

Chapter Fourteen:
We Made It Through All That Other Stuff...Onward!

Whew, I know it could have been a bumpy ride by now, but you've made it through all that initial documentation and are now just living life. However, your spouse may only have a Green Card, which is usually fine. However, if you strive to go further and seek full citizenship, you or your spouse can undergo the Naturalization process, as briefly discussed in Chapter 8.

What is Naturalization?

Naturalization is the legal process by which a foreign national becomes a U.S. citizen. It is governed by federal law and administered by USCIS. The process involves several steps to ensure that applicants meet all eligibility criteria and understand the rights and responsibilities associated with U.S. citizenship.

Determine if You Are Already a U.S. Citizen

Before applying, it's essential to determine whether you may already be a U.S. citizen by birth or through your parents. This could save time and prevent unnecessary applications. It may seem obvious that you would know if you were a citizen or not, but not everyone has the same experience; there could be multiple situations where you may not be aware of your citizenship status.

- **Citizenship by Birth**: Anyone born in the U.S. or certain U.S. territories is automatically a U.S. citizen.
- **Citizenship Through Parents**: If one or both parents were U.S. citizens at birth abroad, you may have automatically acquired citizenship.
- **Derivative Citizenship**: Children under 18 may become citizens automatically if their parent naturalizes and certain conditions are met.

If there is any doubt, applicants should seek clarification through USCIS or consult an immigration attorney.

Check Your Eligibility Requirements

To apply for naturalization, you must:

- **Be at least 18** when filing Form N-400, Application for Naturalization.
- **Be a lawful permanent resident (LPR)** of the United States for at least 5 years (or 3 years if married to a U.S. citizen).
- **Have continuous residence** in the U.S. as an LPR for at least 5 years immediately preceding the application date.
- **Be physically present** in the U.S. for at least 30 months out of the 5 years immediately preceding the application date.

- **Demonstrate good moral character,** including adherence to U.S. laws.
- **Be able to read, write, and speak basic English,** unless exempt due to age and long-term residency or a qualifying disability.
- **Pass a civics test** covering U.S. history and government, unless exempt

Prepare and Submit Form N-400

Complete Form N-400, Application for Naturalization, available on the USCIS website. Gather required documents, such as:

- *A copy of your Permanent Resident Card (Green Card).*
- *Passport-style photographs (if residing outside the US).*
- *Evidence of marital status, if applicable.*
- *Proof of military service, if applicable.*

Submit the form online or by mail, along with the appropriate filing fee. Submit the form online or by mail, with the current filing fee. Fee waivers or reductions may be available for qualifying applicants. Form N-400 is the official application.

It requires applicants to disclose a wide range of information:

- *Biographic details (name, address, birthdate).*
- *Travel history (all trips outside the U.S. during the last 5 years).*
- *Employment and residential history.*
- *Marital history.*
- *Information about children.*

- *Criminal background (if any).*

Supporting Documentation Includes:

- **Green Card (Form I-551)** – front and back copies.
- **Marriage certificate** (if applying based on marriage to a U.S. citizen).
- **Proof of spouse's U.S. citizenship**, such as birth or naturalization certificates.
- **Tax records, child support documents, arrest records**, or other documentation as relevant.

Filing Process:

- Applicants may file **online** through a USCIS account or **by mail** to the appropriate lockbox.
- As of 2025, the fee is **$710** if you file online or **$760** by paper. **No separate biometrics fee applies.**
- **Fee waivers** are available via Form I-912 for those who qualify based on income or financial hardship.

USCIS offers a reduced naturalization fee for certain applicants based on their income; please review the current guidance before filing.

When to file: You may file up to **90 days** before you complete the 3- or 5-year continuous residence requirement.

Attend Biometrics Appointment

After submitting your application, USCIS may schedule a biometrics appointment to collect fingerprints, photographs, and signatures. This information is used to conduct background checks. Usually, around 3–5 weeks after submitting Form N-400,

USCIS sends a **Notice of Action (Form I-797C)** for a biometrics appointment.

What Happens:

- You will go to a **USCIS Application Support Center (ASC)**.
- USCIS collects **fingerprints, a photo, and a digital signature.**
- Biometrics are used for an **FBI background check.**
- Bring the appointment notice and a valid ID (e.g., passport, green card, or state ID).

Complete the Naturalization Interview

The next step is the **naturalization interview**, typically scheduled 6 to 12 months after the application is submitted. USCIS will schedule an interview to review your application and assess your eligibility. Another note here: Arwa's interview for naturalization took place at the U.S. Consular Office in the Kingdom of Bahrain, overseas. So, do not fret; you can complete this process almost anywhere in the world, as long as there is a U.S. Consular office near you.

During the interview, you will be tested on:

- **English language proficiency**: Reading, writing, and speaking.
- **Civics knowledge**: U.S. history and government.

Applicants may be eligible for accommodation or exemptions based on age, long-term residency, or disability.

Notification:

- USCIS sends a letter with your interview date, time, and location.

At the Interview:

- A USCIS officer will review your entire N-400 application.
- You must answer questions under oath and verify details.
- You'll take the **English and Civics tests**, unless exempt.

English and Civics Tests Details:

1. *Speaking: Evaluated during the N-400 interview.*
2. *Reading: Read one out of three sentences correctly.*
3. *Writing: Write one out of three sentences correctly.*

Civics Test:

- You'll be asked 10 questions from a list of 100.
- You must answer at least six questions correctly to pass.
- USCIS provides a complete study guide online.

Accommodations:

- If you are over **50 years old and have lived in the U.S. for 20 years**, or over **55 with 15 years**, you may take the civics test in your native language.

NOTE: This section is crucial for individuals seeking to bring their family to the U.S.. As you can see, the final test is not all that difficult. Arwa took this test, and although studying for it may seem daunting, it is nothing to be afraid of. You and your partner can easily get through this test by learning together.

Your spouse will have to take the test independently, but trust me, it is not that difficult. If your family members are older and speak a different language, there is even accommodation for them to take the test in that language. This is particularly important for non-native English speakers.

Applicants with disabilities may request exemptions by completing Form N-648, which a medical professional must sign.

Await USCIS Decision

After the interview, USCIS will issue a decision:

- **Granted**: Your application is approved.
- **Continued**: Additional information or documentation is required.
- **Denied**: Your application is rejected due to ineligibility.
- You can request a hearing using **Form N-336** if your application is rejected.

Take the Oath of Allegiance

If approved, you will be scheduled for a naturalization ceremony. During this ceremony, you will take the Oath of Allegiance, renouncing allegiance to any foreign state and pledging loyalty to the United States. Upon taking the oath, you will receive a Certificate of Naturalization, officially becoming a U.S. citizen.

Taking the **Oath of Allegiance** is the final step to becoming a U.S. citizen.

Oath Ceremony:

- USCIS sends Form N-445, **Notice of Naturalization Oath Ceremony.**
- Ceremonies may be held at USCIS field offices or other venues.
- You'll return your Green Card and receive a **Certificate of Naturalization.**

The Oath:

"I hereby declare, on oath, that I absolutely and entirely renounce and abjure all allegiance and fidelity to any foreign prince, potentate, state, or sovereignty... that I will support and defend the Constitution and laws of the United States of America..."

Post-Oath Checklist:

- Register to vote.
- Apply for a U.S. passport.
- Update Social Security records.
- Petition for family members, if eligible.

Rights and Responsibilities of U.S. Citizens

As a U.S. citizen, you are entitled to:

- *The right to vote in federal, state, and local elections.*
- *Eligibility for federal employment and government benefits.*
- *The ability to apply for a U.S. passport and travel freely.*
- *Protection and assistance from U.S. embassies and consulates abroad.*

Responsibilities include:

- *Obeying all U.S. laws.*
- *Serving on a jury when called.*
- *Registering with the Selective Service (for male citizens aged 18-25).*

- *Participating in the democratic process through voting and civic engagement.*

Special Considerations and Exceptions

Certain applicants may qualify for exceptions or accommodations:

- **Military Personnel**: Members of the U.S. Armed Forces may be eligible for expedited naturalization.
- **Age and Residency Exemptions**: Applicants 65 or older with 20 years as an LPR study a shorter civics list and can test in their native language.
- **Disability Waivers**: Applicants with physical, developmental, or mental disabilities may request exemptions from the English and civics requirements by submitting Form N-648, Medical Certification for Disability Exceptions.

The naturalization process is a pathway to full participation in American civic life. By understanding the eligibility requirements and following the steps outlined by USCIS, applicants can successfully navigate this process. For personal assistance, consider consulting an immigration attorney or accredited representative.

Children, Birth Abroad, and Citizenship

Raising a family is one of the most important parts of this journey. Paperwork is essential, yes, but the whole point of crossing oceans and paying fees is to build a home together. For us we had our second child abroad, born in the Kingdom of Bahrain. In places like that, you must be married first before having any children. Some locations, such as Bahrain, have strict guidelines about what happens if an unwed mother gives birth.

And it is not fun or happy, but that is the law in that country; be very careful in this regard. So, if the home you are building includes children, and if a birth may happen outside the United States, there are a few things you should know now rather than later. Remember: None of this constitutes legal advice. Rules change, and every family has its own unique circumstances. However, this will provide you with a clear path to follow and the right questions to ask.

Who Is a U.S. Citizen at Birth When the Child Is Born Abroad

Start with the basics. Some children born outside the United States are U.S. citizens the moment they are born. Others are not citizens at birth, but there are clean paths to citizenship later. Whether a child is a citizen at birth depends on the parents' citizenship, their marital status at the time of birth, and the amount of time the U.S. citizen parent has spent living in the United States before the child's birth.

Married parents, both U.S. citizens:

If both of you are U.S. citizens and you are married to each other when the child is born, the child is a U.S. citizen at birth as long as at least one parent lived in the United States at some point before the birth. There is no specific number of years in that scenario. You will still need to document it, which we will cover in the following section.

Married parents, one U.S. citizen and one noncitizen:

Suppose only one of you is a U.S. citizen, and you are married at the time of birth. In that case, the U.S. citizen parent usually must have a certain amount of prior physical presence in the United States before the birth. For children born in recent decades, the rule is five years in total, with at least two of those years after the U.S. citizen turned 14. Time spent abroad while serving honorably in the U.S. military, or working for the U.S. government or specific international organizations, can be counted as if it were time spent in the United States. Please keep a record of that time, as you will be asked for it.

Unmarried parents:

The law treats this differently. You can still transmit citizenship at birth in many cases, but there are extra steps and proofs, such as paternity and acknowledgement of support for a child born to a U.S. citizen father who is not married to the mother. The required amount of prior physical presence for the U.S. citizen parent generally matches the five-year rule mentioned above for births in recent decades. If this is your situation, read the embassy's page carefully and consider consulting a qualified attorney to review your facts.

Assisted reproduction and surrogacy: families are made in different ways. Today, if the parents are married, and at least one parent has a genetic or gestational connection to the child, the child can be treated as born in wedlock for citizenship purposes. You will need to demonstrate a legal parent-child relationship and provide evidence of a biological or gestational link. Consular officers may request medical records, contracts, or other documentation, and in rare cases, a DNA test.

A quick reminder on tone and expectations is in order here. Consular officers are not trying to pick apart your family for sport. Their job is to apply the law and record the facts. Go in prepared and calm, carry clean copies of everything they asked for, and answer questions directly.

How To Document a Birth Abroad

The Consular Report of Birth Abroad, commonly referred to as a CRBA, is the document that records the birth of a U.S.

citizen outside the United States. This is the gold standard record for a citizen child born overseas. Here is the flow most families follow.

Timing: Apply as soon as possible after the birth, and before the child's 18th birthday. Earlier is better. Some posts allow you to start the case online, upload scans, and pay the fee, then finish at an in-person appointment. Other posts handle it entirely by appointment. The embassy website for your country will spell out the local process.

Forms: You will complete an application for the CRBA and a passport application for the child. It makes sense to apply for the CRBA and the first U.S. passport on the same visit. You can also ask for a Social Security number later, either through the local Federal Benefits Unit or after you arrive in the United States.

Who must attend: the child must appear, and usually both parents must appear in person. If one parent cannot participate, read the embassy instructions for consent options and forms. Some posts will accept a notarized consent from the absent parent.

Documents to bring: check the embassy list and match it exactly. In general, you should expect to get the child's local birth certificate and a certified translation if it is not in English, proof of the U.S. citizen parent's citizenship and identity, evidence of the parents' marriage and termination of any prior marriages, and proof of the U.S. citizen parent's physical presence in the United States for the required period. For physical presence, bring what you have from the years before birth. **Tax transcripts, W-2s, school transcripts, leases, utility bills, pay stubs, medical records, entry and exit stamps, and travel itineraries can all be helpful.** If you are counting time abroad due to military or

U.S. government service, bring orders and proof of service. For assisted reproduction or surrogacy, get the medical and legal documents that show the relationship.

Photographs and names: bring passport photos for the baby that meet the current rules. Decide on the child's full name in the order you will use in both countries. Different alphabets and naming customs can cause headaches later, so try to make the records match.

Interview day: you will hand in your documents, answer questions about your relationship and time in the United States, and sign the forms. Suppose the officer believes DNA testing is necessary to prove a claimed relationship. In that case, you will be instructed on how to arrange it using an approved laboratory and chain of custody procedures. Avoid attempting to pre-arrange your DNA testing with a random lab. Wait for instructions if it is requested.

What you receive: once approved, you will receive the CRBA and the child's U.S. passport. Keep the originals in a safe place. Order certified copies if the post office offers that option. The CRBA does not expire. The passport will have the standard validity for a minor and will need to be renewed later.

Two-Parent Consent Rules for Passports

For children under 16, both parents generally must consent to the issuance of a U.S. passport. If one parent cannot attend, you will need a signed and notarized consent form from the absent parent, along with a copy of the ID they used when signing. If one parent cannot be located, a court order is in place, or there are urgent travel needs, read the exceptions carefully. The officers at post will follow those rules closely, and having the proper consent document saves you from repeat trips.

If You Missed the CRBA Window or the Child Was Not a Citizen at Birth

Families move a lot. Sometimes, years pass, and you realize you never applied for the CRBA. If your child was a U.S. citizen at birth, you can still prove citizenship later. A U.S. passport serves as proof. You can also request a Certificate of Citizenship from USCIS inside the United States. The CRBA itself is only available before the age of 18, so after that, you will need to choose between a passport or a certificate as proof of citizenship.

If your child did not acquire citizenship at birth, there are still good paths.

Automatic citizenship in the United States: A child can automatically become a U.S. citizen after birth under the law if certain conditions are met. The child must be under 18, must live in the United States as a lawful permanent resident, and must be in the legal and physical custody of a U.S. citizen parent. When all these conditions are met simultaneously, the child becomes a citizen automatically. Many families then apply for a U.S. passport for the child or file for a Certificate of Citizenship to establish a paper record.

Citizenship while living outside the United States: If a child lives abroad with a U.S. citizen parent and is not a citizen already, a separate application is available that can lead to citizenship through an interview and oath in the United States. That route allows you to count the U.S. physical presence of a U.S. citizen grandparent if the U.S. citizen parent does not have enough time. This is a helpful option for families who will not be relocating to the United States anytime soon.

Adoption: Adoption cases have their own rules, which depend on the type of adoption and the visa route used. If adoption is on your horizon, read early and talk to a qualified professional. It is very doable with good planning.

Dual Nationality and Travel with Kids

Many children born abroad are citizens of two countries. That can be a gift, and it can also be confusing. The United States requires a U.S. citizen to use a U.S. passport to enter and leave the country. The other country will often expect the child to use that country's passport to enter there. Carry both when you travel and use the passport that matches the border you are crossing.

Some countries treat dual nationals as citizens of only one country once you are inside their borders, which can affect how their local laws apply to you and your child. If your child holds the other country's citizenship, read the local rules on things like exit requirements, military service, and parental consent for travel. None of this is meant to scare you. It is simply smarter to know the rules before you fly.

Name differences can be a real source of trouble in dual-nationality families. Different alphabets, hyphens that vanish on a local birth certificate, or a missing middle name in one record can slow down future renewals. Try to keep the U.S. records and the foreign records aligned. If the order of names must differ due to local law, maintain a folder that explains the difference, along with copies of both relevant government documents.

Practical Steps After a Birth Abroad

Health insurance: If you have employer coverage in the United States, add the child to your plan within the enrollment window. If you are stationed abroad or working for a U.S. employer, ask the plan administrator how to add a newborn who has foreign birth documents. If you are using a local plan, keep the policy and claim records on file. You will need them if you switch plans later.

Social Security number: Once you have the CRBA and the passport, ask the local Federal Benefits Unit whether they can process the Social Security number request. If not, visit the Social Security office upon arrival in the United States with the child. Bring the CRBA, the passport, and proof of the parents' identities.

Taxes: if the child is a U.S. citizen, even if living abroad, they are considered a U.S. person for tax purposes. Consult with a preparer who is familiar with expat tax rules if you reside outside the United States. Please **note** that you will need a Social Security number for certain credits and a clean tax return. If you are filing from overseas, keep copies of everything you send.

Schools and records: keep several certified copies of the CRBA and the local birth certificate. Schools, sports leagues, and agencies sometimes ask for them. If the foreign birth certificate is in a language other than English, keep a certified translation with it. Try to keep one spare set of originals in a safe, separate location from the copies you carry.

A Few Field Notes from Our House

We have moved a few times and have had our share of paperwork days with tired kids in tow. The things that helped us most were simple. We kept one clear folder for each child with a checklist taped inside the cover. We wrote down which documents were in the folder and which were stored in the safe. We made a habit of updating the folder once a year, around the time we renewed the kids' passports or when school started.

For name choices, we sat down and wrote the full name in the order it would appear in both countries. We checked how the local registry would print it and how the U.S. passport would print it. Matching them saved us extra questions later.

We also learned to take our time with the physical presence proof for the CRBA. It is not enough to say you lived in the United States. Bring tangible, dated papers that show you were there. If you are in the military or government, your orders and service records are your most valuable assets. If you are not, your school records, tax transcripts, and leases may be the backbone of your file.

Checklist You Can Tackle Now

Before pregnancy or early in pregnancy

- Read the embassy page for the country where the birth may happen.
- Make a simple list of the U.S. citizen parent's time in the United States. Gather proof now, while it is easy to find.
- Decide how you want the child's full name to appear in both legal systems.

Right after birth

- Order the local birth certificate and a certified translation if needed.
- Book the CRBA and passport appointment. If the post uses an online system, create an account and upload the scans they request.
- Gather proof of the U.S. citizen parent's physical presence in the United States, proof of citizenship, marriage documents, and any adoption or assisted reproduction papers.

- Take compliant passport photos for the baby.

At the appointment

- Bring the child and both parents if possible.
- Bring originals and copies of every requested document. Label them in the same order as the embassy checklist.
- Answer questions truthfully. If DNA testing is requested, follow the officer's instructions for the approved lab and process.

After approval

- Store the CRBA and the passport in a safe place. Keep certified copies if offered.
- Apply for the Social Security number through the Federal Benefits Unit if available, or plan to visit SSA in the United States.
- Add the child to your health insurance.

If you discovered later that you missed something

- If the child was a citizen at birth but never got a CRBA, apply for a U.S. passport or a Certificate of Citizenship.
- If the child was not a citizen at birth, look at the rules for automatic citizenship after entry as a permanent resident, or the application route for a child living abroad. Watch the age limits and plan early.

You have done hard things already. This is another season of forms and patience, but it leads to the part that lasts. Children remember steadiness. They remember that you showed up for them, not only on the big days, but also on the quiet days when you gathered papers, stood in line, and made sure their future was settled. Do that work now. It is worth it later when the only papers you are holding are school drawings and permission slips, and the rest of it is tucked away where it belongs.

For more detailed information and resources, visit the official USCIS website: https://www.uscis.gov/citizenship.

Chapter Fifteen:
Final Thoughts

Rounding it all out and breaking it all down is truly a massive undertaking, but we will give it a go. First and foremost, I hope and pray, not the wishy-washy kind, but genuine hope and prayer, that you make it on your journey. There is nothing more satisfying than knowing you at least gave it your best effort. Some of you may stumble along the way, but never get discouraged and never give up on anything; you have invested too much not to keep improving and striving for true maturity in your relationship. There is always, of course, a caveat to that, as some situations just become untenable.

However, we will not focus on that. I want you to put this book down, thinking that there is a chance and hope in the way God gives hope, not that maybe something will happen, but that good things are promised and available for the taking along your K-1 Visa journey.

Keep your focus on what is best for both of you. Take time to listen and understand where your partner is coming from and what they want to accomplish. Give it your all, even if it means losing a little sleep. Please provide them with opportunities to excel and succeed in life, and let them decide whether to take those opportunities or make a different choice entirely.

Speaking of best efforts, I recently had some very enlightening conversations with my brother Joe. He pointed out that even if we think we are doing our best, there is always room for improvement, or some such nonsense, just kidding. As cliché as it sounds, we can always strive for better, but when you are in the moment, you can only work with the information you have at the time, and when you make those decisions in that moment, you are prepared as best you can, then you are doing the best you can.

But as hindsight is always 20/20, it pays dividends in the future to look back and learn from the mistakes and improvements we could have made in those moments. I often find myself leaving conversations thinking, *"Dang it, I could have said this and it would have been much better,"* or *"I could have acknowledged this, and it would have been much more endearing or thoughtful on my part."* But that is life, at least spend the time to reflect on what you can do better the next day.

Also, trust in God. I know that idea exists in many different forms for many other people, but whatever that form is, use it, rely on it, and allow God to guide and calm you. I would say that if your God is not calming you and positively directing you, then maybe it's time to evaluate that relationship. No matter what your situation in life, and I mean even at life's most devastating, or most amazing and life-affirming moments, God should always be a source of strength, power, and positivity in your life-a refuge, despite anything else. And never take the actions of another human being as the actions of God. People, in general, are flawed and tend to look out for themselves; however, this is not the case with a loving and understanding God. The distinction is incredibly stark when you truly put thought into it; there are flawed humans like you and me, and there is God.

Never be afraid to be your true self with your life partner, especially if that person is from a different country. Be honest about who you are, as I mentioned above in the book. It is worth reiterating here that honesty is not only essential for smoothly navigating the K-1 Visa process, but it will also set a solid foundation for you and your partner. Nothing upsets me more about those shows than when someone in one of those TV relationships suddenly has a big secret to reveal, which is likely to ruin the relationship because they decide not to be upfront about it. Just go in with a clear conscience, y'all!

This is what that TV drama trash is: they want to build up the tension and create a super dramatic moment, *"bleh"*. Just be real, and if you are not prepared for this kind of relationship due to finances or job stability or some venereal disease you have, or some whole other family you have that you have not entirely divorced from yet, then do not get involved with this kind of relationship. You are not ready for that kind of commitment, and you will likely bring more pain than pleasure to that relationship.

Remember that this person is giving up a significant part of their life, including people, friends, and family, to be with you. Not respecting that by bringing them into a false situation, although not punishable by law, with a few exceptions, should be punishable. It is a negative mark on your character. I am very adamant about this because I have seen too many people in similar situations, and it needs to stop.

So, look out for your friends and family in these cross-border relationships, make sure they are well-supported, and encourage them to read this book! "Come and get this hot meal", (IYKYK), as a good friend of mine used to say!

Gain some insight into the things that may help them along the way, and as a bonus, guide them through the formal K-1 Visa process. Ask questions in a positive and affirming way, an honest way that lets them know you are there to support them.

For all family members who may be embarking on this journey with a loved one seeking a K-1 Visa, your presence is essential. You need to make sure those people have family to help and guide them. Now, do not try to take over that relationship; instead, ask questions to ensure they are in the right mindset. Be there for their wedding, ensure they have a translator to address any language barriers, take the time to truly learn that language yourself, and help plan out the details for them, but do so lovingly and mutually; remember, it is their relationship. Most importantly, try to understand, embrace, and be open to accepting the person from a foreign country who is coming into your family. Treat them accordingly and *do unto them what you would want done for you.* They are likely scared, unsure, and uncertain; they need to feel wanted and loved. Always start with love, move them in spirit and mind with your kindness and openness, and I can assure you that this will be the most fruitful relationship in your life as a family member to that K-1 Visa couple.

So, go forward with love and respect, and you will never regret being part of a K-1 Visa relationship. Thanks for reading, everyone!

Acknowledgment

First, I thank God for the blessings in my life; nothing is possible without prayer and belief. I'm deeply grateful to my fantastic wife, who has endured much and remained present for our children and me. To my daughters: you're growing into incredible young women. You are talented, funny, resilient, challenging, and insightful. You keep me on my toes and remind me to stay focused so I can help set you on a good path.

Thank you to both our families and to my friend Tim. Without you all, Arwa and I would never have met. To my late friend Jesse Altillio, thank you for serving as our translator and witness at our marriage, helping us move forward together. You're remembered always, brother. Finally, we would like to show our gratitude to our extended friends and family, who are incredibly special to us; you know who you are.

About the Author

Nice to meet you on your journey!

I'm Samuel Beall, the author of this book and the stories that come with it. I decided to use our lives as a living guide to the ups and downs of the K-1 visa process, sharing personal experiences and lessons along the way. You'll notice a strong emphasis on commitment. Not a fashionable kind, but a selfless kind. I hope you find this book helpful and that your journey brings more successes than failures. Nothing will be perfect. I'm excited to see where life leads as our children grow older and head to college. Life gets more interesting when you open yourself to it and surround yourself with good people.

Enjoy the reading!

www.ingramcontent.com/pod-product-compliance
Lightning Source LLC
Chambersburg PA
CBHW062052290426
44109CB00027B/2803